CR   CING

The MIT Press Essential Knowledge Series

CROWDSOURCING

DAREN C. BRABHAM

The MIT Press | Cambridge, Massachusetts | London, England

© 2013 Massachusetts Institute of Technology

MIT Press books may be purchased at special quantity discounts for business or sales promotional use. For information, please email special_sales@ mitpress.mit.edu or write to Special Sales Department, The MIT Press, 55 Hayward Street, Cambridge, MA 02142.

This book was set in Chaparral Pro by the MIT Press. Printed and bound in the United States of America.

Library of Congress Cataloging-in-Publication Data

Brabham, Daren C., 1982–
Crowdsourcing / Daren C. Brabham.
   pages   cm. — (The MIT Press essential knowledge series)
Includes bibliographical references and index.
ISBN 978-0-262-51847-5
1. Human computation. 2. Human-computer interaction. I. Title.
QA76.9.H84B73   2013
004.01'9—dc23
2012045907

10   9   8   7   6   5   4   3   2   1

CONTENTS

SERIES FOREWORD

The MIT Press Essential Knowledge series offers accessible, concise, beautifully produced pocket-size books on topics of current interest. Written by leading thinkers, the books in this series deliver expert overviews of subjects that range from the cultural and the historical to the scientific and the technical.

In today's era of instant information gratification, we have ready access to opinions, rationalizations, and superficial descriptions. Much harder to come by is the foundational knowledge that informs a principled understanding of the world. Essential Knowledge books fill that need. Synthesizing specialized subject matter for nonspecialists and engaging critical topics through fundamentals, each of these compact volumes offers readers a point of access to complex ideas.

Bruce Tidor
Professor of Biological Engineering and Computer Science
Massachusetts Institute of Technology

A friend of mine turned me on to Threadless T-shirts in early 2005 when I was a master's student at the University of Utah. I was a big fan of the shirts and bought a lot of them. Threadless became a staple in my wardrobe, and I loved the concept of how the business worked. As a member of the online community, I could submit T-shirt designs (although I never did), vote on the designs in the gallery, and participate in the vibrant forum discussions on the site.

Friends in Salt Lake City used to ask me about my shirts, and I always overshared my enthusiasm for the site. Pretty soon, they too were buying multiple Threadless shirts, and I felt like an evangelist. I never ran into anyone in Salt Lake City who had already heard of the company before I told them the good word.

Wondering if anyone in the Utah media had written about the company, I searched "Threadless Utah" late one night in early June 2006. At the top of the search results was an article in *Wired* that featured Threadless prominently. Jeff Howe called Threadless's business structure *crowdsourcing*. I suddenly had a word to describe how the company worked, and I learned of similar companies in Howe's article.

After finishing my master's degree with a strong critical-cultural studies focus, I started wondering about how this genius business model could be used for other purposes, particularly in the areas of social justice, democratic participation, and environmental activism. I was about to begin my doctoral work a few months later, and my then-girlfriend, Annie, who is much better at connecting dots than I am, suggested that crowdsourcing—and the pursuit of crowdsourcing to serve the public good—should be the focus of my doctoral work.

I spent my entire doctoral career studying how crowdsourcing worked and crafting arguments for how it could be used as a problem-solving model for public good. My work culminated in a grant-funded project from the Federal Transit Administration, with the generous guidance of Thomas W. Sanchez, to test crowdsourcing in a public-participation program for transit planning. I have enjoyed a research career and a series of consulting engagements focused on crowdsourcing ever since.

In my research, I have watched the term *crowdsourcing* permeate discussions about problem solving. People have planted flags and declared boundaries around crowdsourcing, but few back their claims with empirical data or with rigorous standards for categorization. The empirical research on crowdsourcing is untidy because it is developing within various disciplinary silos that are not in conversation with one another. And when untidy scholarly discourses mix with arbitrary popular media usage about crowdsourcing, the result is unkempt theory and practical crowdsourcing applications with shaky foundations.

This book is an attempt to bring together the big, wandering conversations on crowdsourcing in an easy-to-digest form that is nuanced enough to serve as a springboard for future research and application yet simple enough to serve as an introduction for someone who has just begun to learn about crowdsourcing's promise.

ACKNOWLEDGMENTS

A small crowd of people is to thank for helping move my thinking on crowdsourcing forward. Jeff Howe's original article in *Wired*, his blog, and a few conversations with him over the years were invaluable. I am also grateful for the insights of Karim Lakhani, Hector Postigo, Tom Sanchez, Joy Pierce, Cassandra Van Buren, Tim Larson, and Kurt Ribisl. I have had many opportunities over the years to present my work on crowdsourcing to scholars and practitioners, and the tough questions these groups asked of me sharpened my perspective.

I also acknowledge the support of my wonderful editors at the MIT Press, Marguerite Avery, Deborah Cantor-Adams, and Katie Persons, whose expert eyes made this book much more readable and fair. I also owe a huge debt to supportive family, friends, and my colleagues at UNC–Chapel Hill. And most of all, this book is for Annie Maxfield, my wife and strongest supporter, who is always right about what's worth studying.

One of the most remarkable things to have come out of the so-called Web 2.0 era is not the tools themselves but the ways that new media technologies have redesigned the relationships we have with one another and with organizations. The Internet has long been a place for participatory culture to flourish, but in the early 2000s, we saw for the first time a surge of interest on the part of organizations to leverage the collective intelligence of online communities to serve business goals, improve public participation in governance, design products, and solve problems. Businesses, nonprofit organizations, and government agencies regularly integrate the creative energies of online communities into day-to-day operations, and many organizations have been built entirely from these arrangements. This deliberate blend of bottom-up, open, creative process with top-down organizational goals is called *crowdsourcing*.

Online communities, it turns out, are fertile sources of innovation and genius, and scholarly research on how and why crowdsourcing works has boomed in recent years. Despite this growth in empirical research about crowdsourcing, however, journalists and scholars continue to write about the phenomenon without incorporating these important findings. Part of this has to do with the differing definitions and interpretations of crowdsourcing, and

This deliberate blend of bottom-up, open, creative process with top-down organizational goals is called *crowdsourcing*.

part has to do with the interdisciplinary nature of crowd-sourcing research. It is not easy to tap into what empirical researchers have learned about crowdsourcing. This book aims to tie together these far-flung studies and put forth a single, coherent overview of crowdsourcing that is grounded in research. It is my hope that establishing a solid conceptual foundation for crowdsourcing will focus future research and applications of crowdsourcing on solving some of the world's most pressing problems, accelerating innovation for businesses, and strengthening democratic participation.

Birth and Buzz

In the June 2006 issue of *Wired* magazine, contributing editor Jeff Howe first coined the term *crowdsourcing* in his article "The Rise of Crowdsourcing." He also launched a companion blog around the same time called *Crowdsourcing: Tracking the Rise of the Amateur*. Building on the spirit of James Surowiecki's 2004 book *The Wisdom of Crowds* and other works, Howe described in this article and early blog posts that followed a new organizational form. Companies took functions that once were performed by employees and outsourced the work to others by making an open call to online communities. *Crowdsourcing* was a fitting portmanteau because it morphed two concepts—outsourcing and a crowd of online laborers—to produce an entirely new word. In the article and on his blog, Howe illustrated the phenomenon of crowdsourcing with a number of cases. Four of these cases—Threadless.com, InnoCentive.com, Amazon's Mechanical Turk, and iStockphoto.com—have become early exemplars of the crowdsourcing model in research on the topic.

Like many new terms that appear in a magazine like *Wired*, *crowdsourcing* took off quickly and within days became widely used. Howe wrote on his blog that a Google search for the term *crowdsourcing* went from turning up three results related to the forthcoming article on one day to more than 180,000 results a week later. Today, more than 16,000 results appear in Google Scholar alone, signifying a rapid proliferation of scholarly research on the topic in the span of just six years.

The term *crowdsourcing* was quickly adopted by the popular press and bloggers. Suddenly, new media examples that structurally had nothing to do with crowdsourcing—such as *Wikipedia*, YouTube, Flickr, *Second Life*, open-source software, and blogs—were all called crowdsourcing. Historical examples (such as the Alkali Prize in the 1700s and the *Oxford English Dictionary* in the 1800s) and marketing gimmicks (such as DEWmocracy and Mars's contests to choose new colors of M&Ms) were all conflated with the term. Soon anything that involved large groups of people doing anything was called crowdsourcing. Many of these loud but misguided voices—including *Forbes*, *BusinessWeek*, and countless social media gurus—spread a confusing message about what exactly crowdsourcing was.

What Crowdsourcing Is and Is Not—Strictly Speaking

For the purposes of this book, I define *crowdsourcing* as an online, distributed problem-solving and production model that leverages the collective intelligence of online communities to serve specific organizational goals. Online communities, also called *crowds*, are given the opportunity to respond to crowdsourcing activities promoted by the organization, and they are motivated to respond for a variety of reasons. This precise definition is employed to aid in empirical research on the subject of crowdsourcing and its derivative concepts, though many will continue to blur these distinctions into a single label of "crowdsourcing" to suit their purposes.

Threadless was featured in Jeff Howe's original *Wired* article, and it is celebrated as a powerful example of the crowdsourcing model. Threadless is a clothing company that sells primarily silk-screened graphic T-shirts on its Web site, Threadless.com. Threadless's shirts begin as ideas from members of the Threadless online community, who create their designs within downloadable Photoshop or Illustrator templates available on the Threadless site. These members then upload their designs to a gallery on the Threadless site, and the rest of the Threadless community scores designs in the gallery on a simple zero to five-point scale. After a week in the scoring gallery, some of the designs with the highest scores are printed in Threadless's Chicago headquarters and sold back to the community through a typical online storefront on the site. The winning designers are awarded a $2,000 cash prize and a $500 Threadless gift certificate. For Threadless, this crowdsourcing arrangement is profitable and low-risk. The company draws its product offerings from the crowd and also folds a market-research activity into the process, never printing a shirt to sell without knowing that there is already demand for it among its consumer base.

Crowdsourcing is not limited to graphic design work. At InnoCentive, another crowdsourcing exemplar, companies can post difficult scientific research and development challenges online and offer cash bounties for solutions. Members of InnoCentive's online community offer solutions to the scientific puzzles, and the companies quickly and cheaply gain valuable insights that their in-house scientists might have struggled to attain. And Amazon's Mechanical Turk service lets organizations farm out tasks to an online community of workers cheaply and efficiently, tapping into a workforce that provides language translations, survey responses, information gathering, and other tasks that humans are better qualified to perform than computers.

In crowdsourcing, the locus of control regarding the creative production of goods and ideas exists *between* the organization and the public, a shared process of bottom-up, open creation by the crowd and top-down management by those charged with serving an organization's strategic interests. This sharing of power between an organization and the public makes crowdsourcing distinct from similar creative processes. At Threadless, clothing is designed and produced by an open creative process that the crowd undertakes under the guidance of Threadless's contest rules and requirements, all to serve Threadless's business interests while rewarding the contributions of winning designers. At InnoCentive, an open call for solutions to tough scientific challenges is combined with challenge-specific rules and solution parameters provided by InnoCentive and the companies that post the challenges in pursuit of their strategic interests. And at Mechanical Turk, workers respond to open tasks that are managed by requesting organizations and designed to serve the organization's needs while paying a small amount of money to the worker.

By my definition, then, *Wikipedia* and open-source software projects are not technically crowdsourcing because the commons is organized and produced from the bottom up and its locus of control is in the community. This definition also means that marketing efforts to engage consumers in the selection of a new beverage flavor or candy color by soliciting simple votes do not count as crowdsourcing either, as these practices situate the locus of control primarily within the organization, making minimal use of a community's talents or labor. And I argue in this book that although the underlying concepts of crowdsourcing have existed for centuries, what we today know as crowdsourcing and what we enjoy as the fruits of crowdsourcing did not truly come into being until the widespread adoption of the Internet in the late 1990s and the spread of high-speed connectivity and the cultivation of online participatory culture in the 2000s.

Outline of the Book

This book unfolds in four parts. Chapter 1 defines what crowdsourcing is and what it is not, looking at some related online phenomena that involve online communities and public engagement but that do not meet the requirements for crowdsourcing. An examination of the concepts and theories that drive crowdsourcing follows. I discuss collective intelligence, the wisdom of crowds, problem solving and innovation, and participatory culture and explore some of the best-known cases of crowdsourcing. The chapter concludes with a discussion of the growing interest in crowdfunding as a method for bringing products to market through distributed fundraising and microsponsorship. Crowdfunding and crowdsourcing share many things in common, but crowdfunding, I argue, is best understood as a stand-alone concept.

Chapter 2's organizing typology makes sense of crowdsourcing as a versatile problem-solving model and classifies a number of cases into four primary types. The remainder of this chapter charts the contours of crowdsourcing research across disciplinary boundaries, including the technology focus of crowdsourcing in the computing disciplines, the performance-driven work on crowdsourcing in the business disciplines, the focus on crowds and motivations in the social sciences, and speculative and case-driven work on crowdsourcing across many professional disciplines.

In chapter 3, I survey the major issues of crowdsourcing that have attracted scholarly attention and confronted practitioners engaged in crowdsourcing. These issues include motivations for crowds to participate in crowdsourcing and misconceptions about who actually participates in crowdsourcing applications demographically and professionally. Also discussed in this section are issues of law and ethics, with an emphasis on the efficiency of crowdsourcing and the question of whether crowds are unfairly exploited for their labor.

The final chapter confronts the future of crowdsourcing, both practical applications and future research directions. Future practical applications include the use of crowdsourcing in journalism and for public participation in governance and the role played by mobile technologies in crowdsourcing. Future research agendas will focus on the study of effective online community management, the use of crowdsourcing for large-scale data analysis, and a continued focus on motivations and performance research.

CONCEPTS, THEORIES, AND CASES OF CROWDSOURCING

But here comes brother Thomas; two heads are better than one; let us take his opinion, my love.
—Samuel Foote, *The Nabob*

Crowdsourcing is a story of cooperation, aggregation, teamwork, consensus, and creativity. It is a new arrangement for doing work, but it also is a phenomenon where, when the conditions are right, groups of people can outperform individual experts, outsiders can bring fresh insights to internal problems, and geographically dispersed people can work together to produce policies and designs that are agreeable to most. In this chapter, I explore how and why crowdsourcing works, what some of the most notable cases of crowdsourcing are, and how the curious phenomenon of crowdfunding fits into this landscape.

Drawing Boundaries

By 2008, the first scholarly attempts to define *crowd-sourcing* began to be published in academic journals. These conflicting scholarly definitions explained crowdsourcing according to the participants and reasons for their participation, according to the tools used across different cases, according to common organizational features across several cases, or according to the degree of complexity or degree of user participation. These many attempts to make sense of crowdsourcing led to competing definitions of the phenomenon and different interpretations of what counted as crowdsourcing and what was excluded.

In a 2012 article in the *Journal of Information Science*, Enrique Estellés-Arolas and Fernando González-Ladrón-de-Guevara surveyed the scholarly literature on crowdsourcing and found nearly forty different interpretations of crowdsourcing, with some scholars using different and conflicting definitions for the term even within their own works. After a systematic analysis and validation of these many definitions, they came up with the following comprehensive definition for *crowdsourcing*:

> Crowdsourcing is a type of participative online activity in which an individual, an institution, a non-profit organization, or company proposes to a group

of individuals of varying knowledge, heterogeneity, and number, via a flexible open call, the voluntary undertaking of a task. The undertaking of the task, of variable complexity and modularity, and in which the crowd should participate bringing their work, money, knowledge, and/or experience, always entails mutual benefit. The user will receive the satisfaction of a given type of need, be it economic, social recognition, self-esteem, or the development of individual skills, while the crowdsourcer will obtain and utilize to their advantage what the user has brought to the venture, whose form will depend on the type of activity undertaken.

This definition is wordy but complete. The key ingredients of crowdsourcing, then, according to a few dozen scholars who have published on the topic, are

1. an organization that has a task it needs performed,

2. a community (crowd) that is willing to perform the task voluntarily,

3. an online environment that allows the work to take place and the community to interact with the organization, and

4. mutual benefit for the organization and the community.

For mutual benefit to be enjoyed, I argue, the locus of control in the creation of goods and ideas in crowdsourcing must reside *between* the organization and the community in a shared space that maximizes the benefits of top-down, traditional management with the benefits of bottom-up, open creative production. When the locus of control resides too much on the side of the organization, such as in a "choose the next flavor" marketing contest, the crowd becomes a mere pawn in the organization's overall goals. The benefit in these arrangements is tilted more toward the organization, which may have publicity reasons for claiming to need the crowd's input. On the other end of the spectrum, when the locus of control resides more on the side of the community, such as in *Wikipedia* or open-source software projects, the crowd is self-governing and provides its own strategic goals, and the organization is merely incidental to the work of the crowd. The benefit in these arrangements is tilted more toward the crowd, which may view the organization—if one exists—only as a platform on which to build a common resource. The interplay between crowd and organization is crucial for crowdsourcing because it ensures a mutually beneficial outcome that probably could not have existed without the cocreative efforts of both parties. It is important to understand what crowdsourcing is *not*. Let us examine some of these concepts individually.

The interplay between crowd and organization is crucial for crowdsourcing because it ensures a mutually beneficial outcome that probably could not have existed without the cocreative efforts of both parties.

Commonly Considered to Be Crowdsourcing—but Technically Not Crowdsourcing

Open Source

First, crowdsourcing is not the same as open-source production. Open-source production describes an arrangement in which individuals cooperate to produce a common resource on their own terms, in their own format, as a self-governing community. As individuals improve the common resource, they freely contribute their improvements back to the commons. Open-source software, such as the Mozilla Firefox Web browser, is an illustration of this arrangement. As bugs and security issues arise in the Firefox browser or as new features are desired, individuals in the Firefox community voluntarily program extensions, plug-ins, and new versions of the browser. Once complete, they publish the new Firefox code back to a common Web site, and the improved versions of the product are freely available for use. The Firefox community, like any open-source community, is self-governing and has established community norms, rules, and best practices for handling versioning of the product.

Why is this not considered crowdsourcing? Open-source production is not crowdsourcing because in its intended design, there is no top-down management of the project. In principle, open-source projects are intended to be bottom-up, self-organized collaborations among programmers who work toward a common goal. The day-to-day workings of open-source production are governed by the community and not necessarily by the project or the project sponsor, although in practice, large open-source projects have begun to adopt a more hierarchical, top-down management process. Conceptually, though, open-source production is a departure from the traditional "closed" production in which an organization dictates the design of a product and directs the labor of employees or contractors toward the realization of the design. With open-source production, both process and design are driven by workers. Regarding the creative production of goods and ideas, the locus of control in a traditional, hierarchical, managed process is situated in the organization, whereas in open-source production this locus of control is situated in the laborers who are distributed outside of (or in the absence of) an organization.

Commons-Based Peer Production

Second, crowdsourcing is not what legal scholar Yochai Benkler calls commons-based peer production. A famous example of commons-based peer production is the online encyclopedia *Wikipedia*. For reasons similar to open-source production, *Wikipedia* does not count as crowdsourcing because there is no top-down directive for what encyclopedia articles need to be written or what content those articles must cover. The growth of *Wikipedia* is driven solely by the community of Wikipedians who contribute their labor and intelligence to improve the resource. *Wikipedia* offers a sandbox in which individuals can play. It provides a set of tools—a wiki with a simple markup language—for anyone willing to contribute to the encyclopedia. Beyond the tools, *Wikipedia* does not drive the production of knowledge on the site. That work is generated and governed by the community, all from the bottom up. Regarding the creative production of goods and ideas, the locus of control resides among Wikipedians, not in the *Wikipedia* organization writ large.

Market Research and Brand Engagement

Third, crowdsourcing is not the same as simple voting or market-research campaigns. People who are simply expressing their opinions or casting votes are not engaging in crowdsourcing. An example of this kind of arrangement is Pepsi's DEWmocracy campaign to select a new flavor for its Mountain Dew soda. Pepsi presented a limited number of flavor options to consumers, and the flavor that received the most votes was selected as the new flavor. These kinds of marketing campaigns, which ask consumers to vote on their favorite from a short list of options, are similar to traditional market-research efforts, such as focus groups and taste tests. The only difference is that today these efforts take place on a larger scale because of the reach of the Internet. In contrast to open-source and commons-based peer production, these marketing activities do not count as crowdsourcing because they involve too much top-down control and not enough bottom-up creativity. Organizations have already narrowed down the possible outcomes by the time that people are asked for their input, and often the only permissible input is a simple rating or vote. Asking the crowd to come up with the flavor from scratch *and* select the winning flavor counts as crowdsourcing. But in simple voting or rating, companies give only small amounts of creative or decision power to the crowd, so no crowdsourcing is happening. In this situation, the locus of control regarding the creative production of goods and ideas resides in the organization, not among the consumers.

Crowdsourcing Is Not Old
Fourth, crowdsourcing is not just old wine in new bottles. Many journalists and bloggers have written off crowdsourcing as just the same old offline collaborative process that has happened for many decades or centuries. Some contend that the creation of the *Oxford English Dictionary* in the 1800s was an early instance of crowdsourcing. Through an open call, people were asked to gather English words and their usage and send them to organizers to be indexed in the dictionary. Even earlier than that was the so-called Alkali Prize in the 1700s. Louis XVI of France offered a cash bounty to the public for a better method to

produce alkali, and Nicolas Leblanc came forward with a solution. These monumental achievements in history involved open calls for solutions to solve difficult challenges but were not really instances of crowdsourcing. Although crowdsourcing rests on long-standing problem-solving and collaboration concepts, it is a new phenomenon that relies on the technology of the Internet.

The speed, reach, rich capability, and lowered barriers to entry enabled by the Internet and other new media technologies make crowdsourcing qualitatively different from the open problem-solving and collaborative production processes of yesteryear. Just as the attributes of the Internet fundamentally changed the music industry's business model, legal terrain, and cultural practices of music sharing and mix tapes from its roots in vinyl and cassette tapes, so too has the Internet ramped up collaborative production processes and problem-solving into an entirely different phenomenon called crowdsourcing.

Despite many claims and blanket statements about what crowdsourcing is or is not, crowdsourcing is not just any instance of an online community. It is not a concept that has been around since before the Internet, nor does it take place in any real sense offline. It is not the same as open-source production, not synonymous with open innovation, and not a new word for traditional market research or marketing gimmicks translated to the Internet. Furthermore, crowdsourcing is spelled as one word, as

Jeff Howe originally coined it, and not in the many alternative forms that have proliferated, such as *crowd sourcing*, *crowd-sourcing*, or *CrowdSourcing*.

Crowdsourcing's Underpinnings

The conditions that make crowdsourcing possible are both technical and conceptual. The Internet and other new media technologies provide a technical backbone that props up crowdsourcing applications, and these technologies also give rise to certain attitudes and methods for engagement in a participatory culture. Conceptually, crowdsourcing can be explained through the processes of problem solving and innovation as well as through the group phenomena of collective intelligence and the wisdom of crowds.

The Internet and Participatory Culture

The Internet enables a kind of networked, creative thinking, and this is one of the many reasons that crowdsourcing can exist only online. Tiziana Terranova wrote that the Internet is an ideal technology for distributed thinking because the Internet is "not simply a specific medium but a kind of active implementation of a design technique able to deal with the openness of systems." Other aspects of the Internet that make it an ideal medium for facilitating creative participation include its speed, reach, temporal flexibility, anonymity, interactivity, low barriers to entry, and ability to carry every other form of mediated content.

Regarding speed and reach, the Internet is an instant communications platform on which messages, and thus idea exchanges, can travel so fast along its channels that the medium virtually erases the issue of time and therefore accelerate creative development. Furthermore, the Internet can have a global reach if people have access to technologies. This means that communication can take place between people in different places rapidly. Coupled with the virtual erasure of time, this global character of the Internet also erases space. Communication theorist James W. Carey pondered the cultural transformations and the societal capabilities of communications technologies unmoored from time and space, noting that inventions like the telegraph accomplished this erasure and united nations in common cultural visioning. Taken together, the speed and asynchrony of the Internet make for a temporal flexibility. The medium conforms to the needs and uses of the particular user, converging different speeds and usage patterns together in a collaborative project online that may be either synchronous (in "real time") or asynchronous.

In contrast to the speed and reach of the Internet is the fact that the Internet is also an asynchronous mode. That is, online bulletin board systems and similar applications enable users to post commentary and ideas to a virtual "location" at one point in time. Although the speed of the Internet tends to make users hasty in their online posts, asynchrony allows other users to engage those thoughts at a later time in measured deliberation. Much like the leaving and taking of notes on a bulletin board in a town square, the Internet can foster a sense of ongoing dialog between members of a community without requiring those members to be present at the same time.

Furthermore, the Internet is an anonymous medium. Users are able to develop their own online identities largely on their own terms, or they can choose to remain anonymous entirely. In a chat room or bulletin board system, for example, people can develop whole new personas or design new bodies (or avatars) to represent themselves and their interests. Anonymity is important for online collaboration, especially when people express ideas and opinions to a commons. Research on nonverbal communication has found that body language, position within the space of a room, and small talk work to "script" the power dynamics of a meeting or interaction. In an online environment, people are free to contribute to online discussions and the vetting of ideas without the burden of nonverbal politics or the power inequities at play with embodied forms of difference, such as race, gender, and (dis)ability. Through the possibility for anonymity in participatory functions, the Internet can liberate people from the constraints of identity politics and performative posturing. Users can become, as John Suler claims, "disinhibited" and expressive online.

The Internet is an interactive technology and a site of convergence where all other forms of media can be utilized. Rather than the simple transmission mode of information that is typical with older forms of media (such as the newspaper, radio, and television) and much policy, the Internet encourages ongoing cocreation of new ideas. Content on the Internet is generated through a mix of bottom-up (content from the people) and top-down (content from policymakers, businesses, and media organizations) processes, as opposed to solely a top-down model. For some, the Internet can alienate users from their neighbors interpersonally and allow users to be exploited financially by some companies. In this era of increased content creation, though, Internet users are learning how to broadcast their own ideas, uncover buried information, and remix previous ideas and content into new, innovative forms. Internet users are potentially creative problem solvers.

A final feature of the Internet that enables crowdsourcing to flourish is perhaps the most important. The Internet has lowered barriers to entry for a variety of activities. On one level, the Internet has allowed people to connect because the speed and reach of the Internet break down the barriers of geography and time, bringing people into conversation with one another. But on a more profound level, the Internet has lowered barriers to information, pulling back the curtain on bodies of professional knowledge and increasing access to useful tools that were once inaccessible.

Consider, for example, the photographic imagery crowdsourcing site iStockphoto. Prior to the Internet, those who wanted to become professional photographers—selling stock photos or otherwise—had to take a formal class in school or apprentice with a professional and needed books on the subject from libraries or bookstores. They also needed to purchase professional-quality cameras, film, lighting kits, photo editing software licenses, and other photography equipment. Eventually, they had to establish themselves as freelance photographers, find customers, handle accounting and legal matters, and possibly rent studio space. Those who wanted to enter professional stock photography in pre-Internet days, therefore, faced enormous barriers to entering the profession in terms of technical and artistic knowledge, equipment costs, and business know-how. Today, however, digital cameras are inexpensive and widely available, and even simple models take professional-quality photos. Lessons on how to compose a shot and use lenses and other equipment are freely available on the Internet, in both text and video tutorials. And a site like iStockphoto provides a one-stop shop for aspiring professional stock photographers to show, sell, and earn income from their work. iStockphoto and similar sites have redesigned the professional photography industry with a cheap, royalty-free, online model. Now users encounter fewer hurdles to starting new hobbies and entering creative industries. The Internet and other new media technologies, such as digital cameras, have dramatically lowered the barriers to knowledge and given access to new spaces for creative expression, sharing, interaction, and doing business.

Taken together, these many features of the Internet—speed, reach, temporal flexibility, anonymity, interactivity, convergence, and lowered barriers to entry—enable a participatory culture online. In 2006, media scholar Henry Jenkins and his coauthors published an influential white paper for the MacArthur Foundation on education in a time of participatory culture. They described participatory culture as

> a culture with relatively low barriers to artistic expression and civic engagement, strong support for creating and sharing one's creations, and some type of informal mentorship whereby what is known by the most experienced is passed along to novices. A participatory culture is also one in which members believe their contributions matter, and feel some degree of social connection with one another (at the least they care what other people think about what they have created).

Collaborative problem solving is certainly a key form of participatory culture, and distributed cognition and collective intelligence are important skills that are needed to navigate today's participatory landscape. Although Jenkins and colleagues were writing just before the term *crowdsourcing* was coined, they would have recognized crowdsourcing as a participatory-culture phenomenon.

Creation and sharing are key features of participatory culture, and these features also describe what Tim O'Reilly and others have called *Web 2.0*. The Web 2.0 era in Internet development began in about 2000. Around that time, Internet penetration in many countries reached a point where the majority of the population was online, and many people were online via high-speed connections. This level of penetration and access to high-speed connectivity was important because it signaled a point in Internet history when many people could easily download and upload rich multimedia content. Participation has long been at the core of the Internet, even from its birth in the mid-twentieth century, but at this tipping point in the early 2000s, people were able to create and share large amounts and varieties of content with each other online. Social networking sites blossomed in the Web 2.0 era as well. Through them, content spread easily and widely, and vibrant online communities developed organically around common interests and offline social, geographic, and professional networks. Many of the early crowdsourcing companies and initiatives were started in this nascent period, as their founders capitalized on this articulation of technology, creative energy, and community. The technologies and social relationships that were fostered by those technologies were the fertile ground in which crowdsourcing took root in the early 2000s.

Problem Solving and Innovation
Kevin Dunbar writes that there are four components to problem solving:

> First, there is an initial state. This is the person's state of knowledge at the start of a problem. Second, there is the goal state; this is the goal that the person wishes to achieve. Third are the actions or operations that the problem solver can use to get to the goal state. Fourth, is the task environment that the solver is working in. The task environment consists of the features of the physical environment that can either directly or indirectly constrain or suggest different ways of solving a problem.

Crowdsourcing is a problem-solving model because it enables an organization confronted with a problem and desiring a goal state to scale up the task environment dramatically and enlarge the solver base by opening up the problem to an online community through the Internet. The problem that the crowdsourcing organization needs solved varies, but generally it involves designing a product, cracking a tough scientific problem, reaching consensus on a difficult public issue, or processing large amounts of data with human intelligence. Rather than tackling these problems internally, the organization externalizes the process to the crowd, which brings a large and diverse set of skills, tools, and ideas to bear on the problem. Christian Terwiesch and Yi Xu found that "ideation problems" are suited for broadcasting to an online base of solvers. This means that issues involving the generation of unique designs and ideas are good candidates for opening up to an online community of individuals who might have something to say about the issue.

Seen through the lens of research and development (R&D) programs or product development, *problem solving* might well be synonymous with *innovation*. Research on innovation has a long history, but two closely related branches of innovation studies are pertinent when it comes to crowdsourcing—user innovation and open innovation. In *user innovation*, sometimes called *lead-user innovation*, individuals outside of an organization—say, customers who use a company's product—modify the product to suit their specific needs, and the organization incorporates those modifications into future mass-market iterations. Eric von Hippel notes that the mountain biking industry, for example, developed out of the modifications that enthusiasts made to standard bicycles to navigate rough terrain. The cycling industry accommodated this new sport, in large part because of the inventiveness, improvisation, and experimentation of lead users. Indeed, many extreme sports, whether they are now mainstream or still considered extreme, and the industries that have grown to service those sports developed in this way.

In *open innovation*, which as Henry Chesbrough writes is an extension of user innovation, organizations systematically embrace openness with external stakeholders to develop new products and services. The R&D process in open innovation thus spans the boundary between firm and consumer, and development can be an ongoing, iterative, two-way process. Taking this open innovation to the Internet amplifies it.

Reaching many solvers in their many task environments via the Internet taps into a wide array of diverse cognitive problem-solving heuristics and ways of seeing the world. The diversity that Scott E. Page advocates in collective intelligence includes outsiders or those who have unexpected and fresh ways of approaching and solving a problem. One advantage of openness in problem solving is that nonexpert outsiders have a chance to provide solutions to organizational challenges, sometimes outperforming experts and insiders. Recent research on innovation and problem solving points to technical, social, rank, and site marginality as significant factors in improving problem-solving performance.

A 2010 article by Lars Bo Jeppesen and Karim R. Lakhani in the journal *Organization Science* reported the results of a study of InnoCentive.com participants. Inno-Centive is a scientific research and development company that broadcasts difficult scientific problems to an online community of "solvers" who provide solutions to the challenge for prize money. Jeppesen and Lakhani found that a positive relationship exists between a solver's chance of winning an InnoCentive challenge and a wide distance between the solver's field of technical expertise and the focal field of the problem. That is, a biologist may fare better than a chemist would at solving a chemical engineering problem. They also found that women, who are largely in the outer circle of the scientific establishment, performed significantly better than men at problem solving. This technical and social marginality in open scientific problem solving is an advantage because the perspectives and internal problem-solving heuristics of outsiders allow them to see novel solutions to problems that experts at the center of a scientific domain may not be able to see.

A paper that was delivered by J. Andrei Villarroel and Filipa Reis at CrowdConf 2010 echoed Jeppesen and Lakhani's findings in an internal context. Villarroel and Reis studied a large, multibusiness European communications corporation that used an internal system for employees to generate new ideas for the corporation. They found that those with lower positions in the corporate hierarchy and those located farther away from the corporate headquarters were positively associated with better innovation performance. These two findings—rank marginality and site marginality—suggest that open problem solving and innovation within a large company can have innovative benefits that are similar to those of companies that broadcast problem-solving challenges externally.

Collective Intelligence and the Wisdom of Crowds

An interdisciplinary field of collective-intelligence studies is emerging, and crowdsourcing is frequently included in the discourse on collective intelligence. Media scholar Pierre Lévy conceived of collective intelligence as a "form of universally distributed intelligence, constantly enhanced, coordinated in real time, and resulting in the effective mobilization of skills." The ability to coordinate and network with one another is at the heart of collective intelligence, and the rise of the Internet as a global network that connects individuals with one another in creative, participatory activities has spurred a surge of interest in collective-intelligence studies.

Some research into collective intelligence concerns swarms or hives of insects and animals that cooperate and coordinate to survive, and still other research examines the ways that computer algorithms or robots coordinate to become collectively intelligent. Reviewing the literature on human collective intelligence, however, Juho Salminen found that these studies have focused on three levels of abstraction—the microlevel, the macrolevel, and the ways that microlevel interactions emerge to produce macrolevel effects of collective intelligence. The microlevel concerns the psychological, cognitive, and behavioral factors, including perceived levels of trust and attention, that enable individuals to engage in collective intelligence.

The macrolevel of abstraction in collective-intelligence research focuses on the performance of systems. James Surowiecki calls this phenomenon the "wisdom of crowds," where, under the right conditions, groups of people can outperform even the best individuals or experts. Surowiecki claims that the wisdom of crowds is based on the independence of individuals in a group, the diversity of the group, and the aggregation of their individual outputs rather than the averaging of their collective work. Essentially, too much cooperation, communication, and negotiation among individuals in a group may jeopardize a crowd's ability to become wise. Lu Hong and Scott E. Page have examined the notion of diversity more closely than Surowiecki. In his book *The Difference: How the Power of Diversity Creates Better Groups, Firms, Schools, and Societies*, Page extends Surowiecki's speculations on crowd wisdom to make a more sophisticated claim about diversity in problem-solving environments in general. In some problem-solving situations, the process benefits by having a number of individuals from cognitively diverse perspectives offer their solutions, even if those individuals are not themselves experts.

Crowdsourcing in Action

Crowdsourcing is a flexible model that is applicable to a wide range of activities, from the production of consumer goods and media content to science and policy. In this section, I present a survey of some well-known and lesser known crowdsourcing cases, organized by topic or scope of work.

Crowdsourcing Consumer Goods and Media

Writing on his blog, Jeff Howe has called Threadless one of the exemplar cases of crowdsourcing: "pure, unadulterated (and scalable) crowdsourcing." Based in Chicago and formed in late 2000, Threadless is an online clothing company. As of June 2006, according to Howe, Threadless was "selling 60,000 t-shirts a month, [had] a profit margin of 35 per cent, and [was] on track to gross $18 million in 2006," all with "fewer than 20 employees." *Forbes* reported that Threadless's sales in 2009 topped $30 million.

At Threadless, the ongoing challenge to registered members of the online community is to design and select silk-screen T-shirts. Members can download T-shirt design templates and color palettes for desktop graphics software packages, such as Adobe Illustrator, and create T-shirt design ideas. They then upload the designs to a gallery on the Threadless Web site, where the submissions remain in a contest for a week. Members vote on designs in the gallery during this time on a zero to five-point rating scale. At the end of the week, the highest-rated designs are finalist candidates for printing, and the Threadless staff chooses about five designs to produce each week in large, limited runs. These T-shirts are sold on the site to members in the online community (as well as to unregistered visitors to the site) through a typical online storefront. Threadless awards winning designers $2,000 in cash and $500 in Threadless gift certificates, and when shirts are reprinted, often by popular demand, winning designers receive an additional $500 in cash for each run.

Many other companies have explored this model as a way to create new products and obtain consumer input before they commit to manufacturing. They include the women's shoe company DreamHeels.com, the furniture company Made.com, and the beverage company Vitamin Water's crowdsourcing contest to develop a new flavor from user ideas submitted through Facebook. A traditional clothing or consumer goods company develops prototypes for new products based on extensive market analysis, countless brainstorming sessions with product designers, a series of focus groups and product tests, and a long process of refinement. The up-front investment for traditional companies is enormous, presumably to minimize the risk of a producing product that fails in the marketplace after it is mass produced. Crowdsourcing companies like Threadless rely on consumers to come up with product ideas, to vet those product ideas through essentially an ongoing process of peer review and refinement, and to indicate their willingness to purchase the end result, all before Threadless commits to printing even one shirt. A traditional T-shirt company employs a team of in-house designers or regularly uses a network of freelancers, so the designers' ability to come up with new ideas that will succeed in the market time and time again is limited. Eventually, the team will produce a dud. But when the process is enlarged online in a crowdsourcing arrangement, a potentially limitless number of ideas may turn up, and the integrated voting mechanism helps to ferret out the duds before they are manufactured. Compared to the traditional consumer-goods product-development process, crowdsourcing can generate more and better ideas while integrating market research and lowering the risks to the organization.

The production of media content is not much different from the production of consumer goods. Both involve generating and vetting ideas that make one product or piece of media content stand out in a field of competitors. Since 2006, Doritos has promoted its Crash the Super Bowl contest, which invites people to submit thirty-second television commercials about the Doritos corn chip brand to a Web site. As with Threadless, the online community votes on its favorite ads until an ad with the most votes wins the contest. The winning ads are aired in the high-profile and expensive ad slots during the National Football League's Super Bowl broadcast, and the creators of the winning ads receive a prize package of cash and gifts, including a trip to the Super Bowl. The crowdsourced ads are consistently rated in the five best Super Bowl ads according to *USA Today*'s Ad Meter rankings. Doritos spends a lot of money promoting the contest, and it is unclear whether the costs of promotional efforts and the prize money are less than what Doritos would pay a Madison Avenue ad agency to produce a commercial. The process does allow Doritos to draw on a much larger pool of creative ideas through the Internet, and it knows in advance which ads appeal to consumers before it commits to airing one during the Super Bowl.

Crowdsourcing has also been used to create journalistic media content but with mixed results. Assignment Zero was launched in early 2007 as a collaboration between *Wired* and Jay Rosen's NewAssignment.net. Assignment Zero was intended to be an experiment in crowdsourced journalism that focused on the topic of crowdsourcing, which at the time was a six-month-old term. The goal was to have an online community of volunteer writers and editors produce the most thorough treatment to date of crowdsourcing. Assignment Zero charged the crowd to come up with story ideas, contact interview subjects, write stories, and edit stories written by others, all in the hopes of publishing dozens of high-quality stories about crowdsourcing's many facets. Writing a postmortem on the project in *Wired* in July 2007, Jeff Howe noted the project "suffered from haphazard planning, technological glitches and a general sense of confusion among participants," although Howe maintained an optimistic tone about the future of crowdsourced journalism projects. Rosen claimed that one problem with Assignment Zero was that tasks were not specific or granular enough for volunteers to understand when they visited the site. That is, the crowd was asked to come up with entire stories, from concept to final editing, without enough structure or management from above. Asking a crowd to write a story on a topic is very different from asking a crowd to copyedit a manuscript, do fact-checking, or do background research to identify potential sources for a story. Task decomposition is one way that organizations exert a level of management and control in a process. Without clearly defined, granular tasks for crowds to perform, the locus of control shifts too far into the domain of the crowd, and crowds may not have a clear sense of the strategic purpose of a project or an organization's overall intentions.

Crowdsourcing Science

Crowdsourced science builds on a long tradition of *citizen science*, or the important contributions that are made by amateurs and hobbyists to the advancement of science. Examples of citizen science include the star discoveries of amateur astronomers, the inventions of countless garage tinkers and inventors, and the Audubon Society's bird-counting events, where everyday citizen bird watchers report their findings to chronicle counts and varieties of bird species across the country. Crowdsourced science accelerates these efforts online, allowing organizations to pose specific scientific challenges to crowds for mutual benefit.

InnoCentive is often cited as a crowdsourcing exemplar in this domain of corporate scientific research and development. Founded in 2002 with a significant investment by drug manufacturer Eli Lilly, InnoCentive focuses on providing research and development solutions for a broad range of topic areas, from biomedical and big pharmaceutical concerns to engineering and computer science topics. InnoCentive boasts a community of dozens of client-company "Seekers" and an online community of 165,000 "Solvers." Seeker companies issue difficult scientific challenges to the Solver community, with cash awards ranging from $5,000 to $1 million. According to Karim R. Lakhani, Lars Bo Jeppesen, Peter A. Lohse, and Jill A. Panetta, "[s]olution requirements for the problems are either 'reduction to practice' (RTP) submissions, i.e., requiring experimentally validated solutions, such as actual chemical or biological agents or experimental protocols, or 'paper' submissions, i.e., rationalized theoretical solutions codified through writing." Submitted solutions are never seen by other Solvers; only Seekers pore over submissions. Solvers with winning solutions are awarded the cash bounties, the Seeker company takes ownership of the intellectual property, and InnoCentive receives a fee from the Seeker company for listing the challenge and facilitating the process.

Lakhani and colleagues conducted a statistical analysis of the InnoCentive service between 2001 and 2006. They found that the Solver community was able to solve 29 percent of the problems that the Seekers—all large companies with internal labs and researchers—posted after they were unable to solve these problems internally. Moreover, the results found a positive correlation between the distance that the Solver was from the field in which the problem was presented and the likelihood of creating a successful solution. That is, Solvers on the margins of a disciplinary domain—outsiders to a given problem's domain of specialty—performed better at solving the problem.

The Goldcorp Challenge was a similar scientific crowdsourcing case. Goldcorp, a Canadian gold mining company, developed the Challenge in March 2000. According to a company press release, "participants from around the world were encouraged to examine the geologic data [from Goldcorp's newly acquired Red Lake Mine in Ontario] and submit proposals identifying potential targets where the next six million ounces of gold will be found." By offering more than $500,000 in prize money to twenty-five top finalists who identified the most gold deposits, Goldcorp attracted more than 475,000 hits to the Challenge's Web site, and "more than 1,400 online prospectors from

51 countries registered as Challenge participants." The numerous solutions from the crowd confirmed many of Goldcorp's suspected deposits and identified several new ones for a total of 110 deposits.

Crowdsourcing may also help scientists refine their research projects by relying on crowds to identify variables for modeling various attitudes and behaviors toward any number of health or prosocial topics. Josh C. Bongard, Paul D. H. Hines, Dylan Conger, Peter Hurd, and Zhenyu Lu tested a system whereby users answered questions about obesity and electricity use, including their body mass index numbers, their electricity usage, and their behaviors associated with these two facets of their lives. Users, in turn, were able to propose new questions about behaviors for future users to answer. Over time, the sophistication of the system was improved with greater participation, and users essentially proposed new behaviors to model against their actual body mass index numbers and electricity usage. By crowdsourcing the generation of variables for behavioral modeling in conjunction with gathering data for these models, the users were contributing to the refinement of behavioral modeling that could be useful for public health practitioners and environmental policymakers.

Crowdsourcing Space and Place

Because crowdsourcing involves an organization that reaches out to a crowd distributed across the Internet and located in many different geographic locations, the model lends itself to addressing challenges of space and place. With crowdsourcing, an organization has an opportunity to gather place-based intelligence from individuals in the crowd, and a number of cases illustrate how this is taking shape in a variety of contexts.

SeeClickFix.com is a Web site that allows people to report nonemergency problems in their local community by using either the SeeClickFix Web site or a free mobile phone application. These problems include potholes, graffiti, malfunctioning traffic signals, obstructed wheelchair access ramps on sidewalks, and other issues of disrepair and public safety. City governments and journalists use SeeClickFix as an intelligence-gathering mechanism for helping them understand the issues facing a community and allocate resources to fix the problems. According to a SeeClickFix spokesperson, "on average, more than 40 percent of issues reported on the site get resolved." SeeClickFix provides an open call for citizens to engage governments efficiently regarding their problems, and it provides an opportunity for government to deliver services to citizens based on that place-based intelligence.

Ushahidi.com is a concept similar to SeeClickFix and focuses instead on mapping issues of concern to social activists and government watchdog groups. Swahili for *witness* or *testimony*, Ushahidi was established after the 2007 presidential election in Kenya, which was widely disputed as fraudulent and led to violence against certain ethnic groups in the country. The Ushahidi platform enabled Kenyans to report instances of ethnic violence via e-mail or text message, and a map of these reports allowed activists and peacemakers to track the path of violent outbreaks efficiently. Ushahidi has subsequently been used to map other crises, natural disasters, protests, and even wireless coverage, providing government officials, activists, first responders, and journalists with useful on-the-ground intelligence.

Crowdsourcing can also allow citizens to reimagine physical spaces to plan collectively the built environment. Next Stop Design was an effort in 2009 and 2010 to crowdsource public participation for transit planning, beginning with a competition to design a better bus stop shelter for the Utah Transit Authority bus system in Salt Lake City. Patterned after sites like Threadless, the project, funded by the US Federal Transit Administration, allowed participants to upload bus stop shelter designs to a gallery on the Next Stop Design Web site and then to rate the designs of peers in the gallery. The three designs with the highest average score at the close of the four-month competition were declared the winners. Without any monetary incentive or promise to construct the winning designs, nearly 3,200 registered users submitted 260 bus stop shelter designs in the competition. Projects like inTeractive Somerville in Somerville, Massachusetts, have built on the crowdsourcing concept to engage citizens in public-participation activities for urban planning and mass transit, and firms like Cooltown Beta Communities enable what they call "crowdsourced placemaking," giving citizens and developers the tools they need to build successful urban cultural districts through a crowdsourcing process.

Crowdsourcing Policy

Governments have slowly warmed up to the thought of using the Internet for public engagement and policymaking. The city of Santa Monica, California, launched the Public Electronic Network in early 1989. It was the first online network operated by a city government for use by the public, and its members used the opportunity to voice concerns and offer solutions to the city's problems. In 2007, New Zealand allowed citizens the chance to craft the wording of the Policing Act through a wiki. And in the wake of a financial collapse in 2011, the government of Iceland used social media to solicit ideas from citizens in the creation of a new constitution. Crowdsourcing as a method for public participation in governance has gained in popularity in recent years, allowing governments to seek the ideas and opinions of citizens on policies and waste reduction.

Peer-to-Patent was a pilot project from 2007 to 2009 between New York Law School and the US Patent and Trademark Office (USPTO), with support from a number of major corporate patent holders. In the Peer-to-Patent project, the USPTO siphoned off a small number of patent applications to an online community. Working for no monetary reward, this online community of more than 2,600 reviewed applications for evidence of "prior art." Prior art is any evidence that a similar invention already exists that would negate the originality of a patent application. These findings were then routed back to the USPTO. Overburdened and backlogged with patent applications, the USPTO then used these findings to help determine whether new patents should be awarded. In 2009, Peer-to-Patent reported that the USPTO used the online community's prior-art submissions to reject one or more claims in eighteen different patent applications, and 69 percent of participating USPTO patent examiners think that a program like Peer-to-Patent would be useful if incorporated in regular practice. Based on the success of the first pilot, another pilot round of the project ran from 2010 to 2011, the project has spread to other countries, and there are plans to continue the project on a permanent basis in the United States. Peer-to-Patent is evidence that the government can effectively mobilize citizens to solve specific problems through a crowdsourcing arrangement.

With the US Office of Management and Budget, President Obama started the Securing Americans Value and Efficiency (SAVE) Award with an eye toward identifying novel solutions for reducing wasteful government spending.

Federal employees were given the opportunity to submit cost-cutting ideas, and the best idea was awarded a prize. In the past two years, more than 56,000 ideas have been submitted by federal employees, and the winning ideas are projected to save the government millions of dollars long-term. In this situation, the US government sought novel, provable solutions from its employees by broadcasting a call for ideas to reduce costs.

Crowdsourcing Microtasks
In its simplest form, crowdsourcing is a way to connect organizations to potential laborers via the Internet. Crowdsourcing appears to be an especially good method for assigning small bits of work called *microtasks* across the Internet. At Mechanical Turk, "Requesters" can use the site to coordinate a series of simple tasks they need to be accomplished by humans. These are tasks that computers cannot do easily, such as accurately tag the content of images on the Internet for a search engine. Individuals in the Mechanical Turk community, known as "Turkers," can sign up to accomplish a series of these *human-intelligence tasks* (HITs), and the Requester pays them very small monetary rewards (often one cent to fifty cents per task). Mechanical Turk essentially coordinates large-scale collections of simple tasks requiring human intelligence, and organizations that use this service acquire important data analysis quickly and inexpensively.

This kind of microtasking has been used in other cases. For example, until its sudden closure in mid-2012, Subvert and Profit used this format to coordinate the gaming of social media sites such as Digg and StumbleUpon. Confidential clients paid Subvert and Profit to distribute rating tasks for certain stories and Web sites to a crowd of registered users, who could make small amounts of money for performing the tasks. Calling their product "social media optimization," Subvert and Profit claimed to have placed thousands of content items on the front pages of high-traffic sites like Digg, resulting in millions of views for paid items. On its site, the company estimated its method was "30 to 100 times more cost effective than conventional Internet advertising."

Making Sense of Crowdfunding
As the related concept of crowdfunding has risen in popularity, researchers have started to examine its participants and methods. *Crowdfunding* describes a funding model whereby individuals use the Internet to contribute relatively small amounts of money to support the creation of a specific product or the investment in a specific business idea. Kickstarter.com is a well-known illustration of the crowdfunding model. At Kickstarter, musicians, artists, filmmakers, and other creative people post an idea for a creative project and ask members in the online community to support the idea with cash contributions. Artists offer a

range of creative rewards to potential investors on the site. For example, filmmakers who want to fund the production of a feature film may pitch an idea on a Kickstarter started page to seek funding from the crowd. A filmmaker may offer a menu of rewards for different levels of support, all of which will be fulfilled if the project reaches its full funding goal. For $20, funders might receive a DVD copy of the final film; for $100, they might be mentioned in the film's credits; and for $500, they might be given a private screening of the film in their home. When filmmakers reach their target fundraising goal, they produce the film, and their many investors are rewarded for their support. The model helps many artistic ideas come into being and engages investors in the support of artistic endeavors they believe in. The model also works for start-up businesses that are seeking crowdfunding to supplement small business loans and angel investors.

However, crowdfunding does not fit the strict definition of crowdsourcing. Crowdsourcing is a blend of top-down managed process and bottom-up open process, with the locus of control over production residing with both the organization and the crowd in a shared, give-and-take way. Crowdfunding does not resemble this structure. In crowdfunding, an artist or an entrepreneur develops an idea and seeks monetary support to bring his or her idea to market. There is no engagement with the crowd on what the artistic endeavor will look like or how the start-up business will be run. Crowdfunding is distributed financing or group investing, not crowdsourcing. Even with Mechanical Turk, which invites crowds to perform simple human-intelligence tasks for pay, members of the crowd contribute their talent and intellect to the work. With crowdfunding, no creative energy or human intelligence is brought to bear on the product itself. Rather, the intellect required of the crowd in a crowdfunding arrangement is to choose a product to support. The relationship to the means of production is different in crowdfunding and crowdsourcing.

Although crowdfunding may not fit the definition for crowdsourcing, it certainly will play a role in the future of product development and will affect creative professions and possibly government funding of the arts in the future. Crowdfunding may help lift independent artists out of obscurity, place them on larger stages, and connect them with patrons through unique reward packages, creating vibrant and loyal online brand communities and providing an alternative to the formulaic plots and predictable sequels of many mass-market films. But governments may begin to see crowdfunding as a viable alternative to public funding of the arts, which has come under scrutiny in the United States and abroad in the wake of economic recession. If small groups of fans are willing to crowdfund these artistic products into being, the political logic may go, then why should taxpayers be expected to foot the bill?

In weak economies, sites like Kickstarter could pose real threats to public arts funding.

However, crowdfunding has the potential to accelerate innovation for the public good, beyond just arts funding, by letting individuals contribute small donations to bring academic research and creative ideas to fruition. Recently, Innovocracy.org was launched to serve academic researchers who have ideas for prototypes that can improve lives, and the site allows individual donors to crowdfund these products into reality. One example is a one-handed control system that stroke survivors who have lost the function of an arm can use to operate a bicycle. The project, developed by a team of researchers at the University of Rochester, sought $6,000 in funding and received more than that amount through Innovocracy's crowdfunding platform. Despite crowdfunding's threat to traditional public funding structures for arts and academic research, it offers creators the speed and flexibility to bring ideas to market through the support of many.

ORGANIZING CROWDSOURCING

There should be a place for everything, and everything in its place.

—Isabella Beeton, *Mrs. Beeton's Book of Household Management*

Crowdsourcing cases can be organized in a four-type typology according to the kinds of problems being addressed. Several academics have offered other typologies for examining crowdsourcing, but here I make a case for why my four-type typology is a more useful lens for viewing crowdsourcing than other typologies. A brief look at the disciplinary interpretations of crowdsourcing research follows, and a concluding policy-advisory framework addresses the management of crowdsourcing applications and organizational commitment to crowdsourcing outcomes.

Organizing Typologies

Many scholars and journalists have categorized aspects of crowdsourcing, including types of crowds, crowdsourcing work, industries served, and functional features. For example, Nicholas Carr proposes a typology of six kinds of crowds rather than applications—social-production crowds, averaging crowds, data-mine crowds, networking crowds, transactional crowds, and event crowds. Carr's crowd typology includes crowdsourcing cases as well as *Wikipedia* and the open-source software project Linux, but he sorts communities based on the kind of labor they perform for various projects and the ways individuals in the crowd communicate and collaborate with one another. This typology is useful for reflecting on the various abilities crowds possess and the many ways they can work together or in isolation to perform labor for an organization, but this categorization does not, in my opinion, provide the level of precision an organization would need to determine if and how to use crowdsourcing to its advantage.

In his 2012 master's thesis, Eric Martineau presented a four-type typology of crowd participation styles, focusing on the motivations of crowds to participate in crowdsourcing applications. He groups individuals in crowds into the following categories—communals, who mesh their identities with the crowd and develop social capital through participation on the site; utilizers, who create social capital by developing their individual skills through the site; aspirers, who help select content in crowdsourcing contests but do not contribute original content themselves; and lurkers, who simply observe. A 2011 paper by Gabriella Kazai, Jaap Kamps, and Natasa Milic-Frayling took a similar approach, offering five worker types for individuals in the crowd—spammer, sloppy, incompetent, competent, and diligent. Although these frameworks are useful for understanding the different levels of engagement that individuals in the crowd may have and the managerial skills that are needed to elicit quality solutions from diverse crowds, these typologies focus more on the crowd members than the problems that crowdsourcing may solve.

Jeff Howe, in his 2008 book *Crowdsourcing: Why the Power of the Crowd Is Driving the Future of Business*, proposed four types of crowdsourcing that focus on the ways that various applications function—through crowd wisdom, crowd creation, crowd voting, and crowd funding. In a 2010 interview with Neil Davey, Ross Dawson offered a similar approach that focused on six functions for crowdsourcing—distributed innovation platforms, idea platforms, innovation prizes, content markets, prediction markets, and competition platforms. In a 2011 article, Eric Schenk and Claude Guittard put forth a nuanced typology based on the integrative or selective nature of the process paired with tasks that are simple, complex, or creative. Also in 2011, David Geiger, Stefan Seedorf, Thimo Schulze,

Robert C. Nickerson, and Martin Schader proposed a more sprawling crowdsourcing classification system that identified nineteen distinct process types based on the intersection of several dimensions.

In 2011, Andrea Wiggins and Kevin Crowston classified various citizen science projects, many of them enabled by the Internet and considered true crowdsourcing projects, according to the kind of activity or purpose that citizens were used by the organization. In other words, the focus is on the kind of problem an organization needs solved when it turns to the crowd. In that problem-centric vein, I propose a typology of crowdsourcing based on four kinds of problems that crowdsourcing is best suited to solve.

The four dominant crowdsourcing types, based on the kind of problems being solved, are the knowledge-discovery and -management approach, the broadcast-search approach, the peer-vetted creative-production approach, and the distributed-human-intelligence tasking approach (see table 2.1).

In the knowledge-discovery and -management approach, online communities are challenged to uncover existing knowledge in the network, thus amplifying the discovery capabilities of an organization with limited resources. The assumption is that a wealth of disorganized knowledge exists "out there" and that a top-down, managed process can efficiently disperse a large online

Table 2.1 A problem-focused crowdsourcing typology

Type	How it works	Kinds of problems	Examples
Knowledge discovery and management	Organization tasks a crowd with finding and collecting information into a common location and format	Ideal for information gathering, organization, and reporting problems, such as the creation of collective resources	Peer-to-patent *peertopatent.org* SeeClickFix *seeclickfix.com*
Broadcast search	Organization tasks a crowd with solving empirical problems	Ideal for ideation problems with empirically provable solutions, such as scientific problems	InnoCentive *innocentive.com* Goldcorp Challenge *Defunct*
Peer-vetted creative production	Organization tasks a crowd with creating and selecting creative ideas	Ideal for ideation problems where solutions are matters of taste or market support, such as design or aesthetic problems	Threadless *threadless.com* Doritos Crash the Super Bowl Contest *crashthesuperbowl.com* Next Stop Design *nextstopdesign.com*
Distributed-human-intelligence tasking	Organization tasks a crowd with analyzing large amounts of information	Ideal for large-scale data analysis where human intelligence is more efficient or effective than computer analysis	Amazon Mechanical Turk *mturk.com* Subvert and Profit *Defunct*

The four dominant crowdsourcing types, based on the kind of problems being solved, are the knowledge-discovery and -management approach, the broadcast-search approach, the peer-vetted creative-production approach, and the distributed-human-intelligence tasking approach.

community of individuals to find specific knowledge and collect it in specific ways in a common repository. This crowdsourcing type resembles commons-based peer production, like the writing and editing done at *Wikipedia*, except that a sponsoring organization determines exactly what information is sought, what its purpose is, and how the information is assembled. In this approach, the more users there are and the more involved they are, the better the system functions, a fact that could be applied to most participatory-culture phenomena. Peer-to-Patent, SeeClickFix, and Ushahidi are examples of the knowledge-discovery and -management approach, and they all address a similar kind of problem. At Peer-to-Patent, the crowd seeks out evidence of prior art via the Internet and submits it to the Peer-to-Patent site to address patent applications. SeeClickFix and Ushahidi operate in a similar way, asking the crowd to find and report instances of urban disrepair or ethnic violence, respectively, to a common mapping interface, which governments then use to allocate city resources or deploy peacekeepers.

Broadcast-search approaches to crowdsourcing are oriented toward finding a single specialist, who probably is outside the direct field of expertise of the problem and who has the time and is able to adapt previous work to produce a solution. In theory, the wider the net cast by the crowdsourcing organization, the more likely the company will turn up the "needle in the haystack"—the one person who knows the answer. The broadcast-search approach is appropriate for problems where a provable, empirically "right" answer exists but is not yet known by an organization. Broadcasting the problem in an open way online draws in potential solutions. Scientific problems, such as developing new chemicals and materials or locating resources for mining using geophysical data, are best suited to the broadcast-search approach. In the broadcast-search approach, monetary rewards are common for individuals in the crowd who provide a solution to a challenge, although financial incentive is not the only motivation for these crowds to participate in these arrangements. InnoCentive and the Goldcorp Challenge use the broadcast-search approach to find scientific solutions to difficult puzzles by casting a wide net online.

With the peer-vetted creative-production approach, the creative phase of a designed product is opened to a network of Internet users, who send in a flood of submissions, including some superior ideas. The peer-vetting process simultaneously identifies the best ideas and collapses the market-research process into an instance of firm-consumer cocreation. It is a system where a "good" solution is also the popular solution that the market will support. Peer-vetted creative production is appropriate for problem solving that concerns matters of taste and user preference, such as aesthetic and design problems. Threadless, Next Stop Design, and user-generated advertising contests, such as the Doritos Crash the Super Bowl Contest, are all examples of the peer-vetted creative-production approach. These are ideation processes where the crowd comes up with creative ideas for products, media content, or designs of physical space. Because the crowd is the eventual user of the product, media content, or space, they are empowered to select the best ideas.

Finally, the distributed-human-intelligence tasking approach to crowdsourcing is appropriate when a corpus of data is known and the problem is not to produce designs, find information, or develop solutions but to process data. It is similar to large-scale distributed-computing projects, such as SETI@home and Rosetta@home, except that it replaces spare computing cycles with humans engaged in short cycles of labor. Large data problems are decomposed into small tasks requiring human intelligence, and individuals in the crowd are compensated for processing the bits of data. Because this crowdsourcing approach is certainly the least creative and intellectually demanding for individuals in the crowd, monetary compensation is a common motivator for participation. Amazon's Mechanical Turk and Subvert and Profit are two examples of distributed-human-intelligence tasking. Each service enables the open distribution of microtasks across the Internet to a community of workers.

Disciplinary Divisions

Research on crowdsourcing has blossomed in a variety of academic disciplines, and each discipline has approached the topic from a different angle. This plethora of approaches has led to some confusion and conflict about what counts as crowdsourcing research, but these many research streams are beginning to merge. The academic disciplines have tended to focus on the few aspects of crowdsourcing that speak to long-running theories, problems, and debates in a given scholarly discourse.

For example, computing research on crowdsourcing to date has focused largely on the design and technical aspects of crowdsourcing systems. Some studies in computing test the performance of existing crowdsourcing systems, some propose hypothetical systems or models for various crowdsourcing applications, and still others report the findings from novel applications or modifications to existing crowdsourcing systems that were designed, built, and tested by scholars or practitioners. The lion's share of research on crowdsourcing has been done in the discipline of computing. This large volume of research can be explained by the brevity of papers in the discipline, the tendency to publish conference papers as proceedings or make them available online quickly, and the fact that entire conferences and workshops have been devoted to the topic of crowdsourcing, bringing larger number of scholars into conversation with one another. These conferences include the International Workshop on Enterprise Crowdsourcing, part of the International Conference on Web Engineering, as well as CrowdConf, a conference sponsored by the enterprise crowdsourcing platform CrowdFlower. Corporate Internet technology research firms, such as IBM Research and HP Labs, are also active in crowdsourcing research from a computing perspective.

However, the volume of crowdsourcing research in the computing discipline is probably best explained by the decades of research into distributed computing and the Internet more generally. The computing discipline already had momentum and precedent for this kind of work and this way of thinking about problems in distributed, collective, and crowdsourced ways. Distributed computing is, simply, the distribution of small parts of a computing problem to different computers on a network. Given a particularly large computational problem that one computer might not be able to handle quickly. it makes sense to decompose the problem into small tasks and assign the tasks to different individual computers that communicate on a shared network. This essentially amplifies computing power in a distributed way and allows a large computational problem to be tackled in a reasonable amount of time. A relatively well-known example of distributed computing is the SETI@home project (SETI standing for the Search for Extra-Terrestrial Intelligence).

A large batch of data from the Arecibo radio telescope is distributed into small chunks across the Internet to volunteers, whose personal computers process the data with an algorithm that searches for patterns and other features that might suggest evidence of alien communication in space. These findings are then communicated back through the network to the SETI@home project computers. Decomposing the enormous data set from Arecibo into portions small enough for personal computers to handle via the Internet assists the project in its search for extraterrestrial life.

In SETI@home and other distributed-computing projects, personal computers on a large network automatically process data using a software program that the volunteer downloads to his or her computer. Not all computing tasks, however, can be handled efficiently by computer algorithms, and human intelligence sometimes is required to process data. If the task is to tag a large set of photos for relevant content, existing algorithms can efficiently detect the size of a photo, the dominant color in the image, and even the number of people present in a photo. But there probably is no algorithm that can easily tag a photo of a person holding open a pizza box as "vegetarian pizza" or "pepperoni pizza," and it would not make sense to write custom code to automate this kind of tagging. A human, however, can easily and quickly figure out the toppings on the pizza and supply an appropriate tag for the image. Taking the principles of problem decomposition in distributed computing and replacing computers in the network with humans produces a hybrid computer-human process that Luis von Ahn (2008) calls "human computation." Large data sets requiring human intelligence can be processed through human computation in much the same way as distributed computing processes large data sets that require only computation. The distributed-human-intelligence tasking type of crowdsourcing and human computation are the same concepts, and research on crowdsourcing from a computing perspective has blended the terminologies and theories of distributed computing, human computation, and crowdsourcing. Much of the work on crowdsourcing in the computing disciplines, however, has taken place in a silo of sorts that is largely disconnected from similar research in other disciplines.

Crowdsourcing research in the computing disciplines has been robust, and some of this high level of research activity can be attributed to the fact that computing is a discipline of designing, doing, and building, as nearly all computer scientists know how to program. Computer scientists who are interested in testing or adding on to an existing crowdsourcing platform or building a new platform are usually equipped to do so. That is, computer scientists who conceive of new crowdsourcing arrangements in theory can actually create and study those arrangements. And the open-source culture of sharing code in the computing world accelerates this iterative cycle of building and studying by computing scholars.

Research on crowdsourcing from a business standpoint has focused on the performance of crowdsourcing applications in terms of innovation, profitability, and efficiency and also on the strategic and managerial dimensions of integrating crowdsourcing into a firm's operations. The performance research on crowdsourcing extends a robust scholarly discourse on innovation and problem solving, especially open innovation and lead-user innovation, which has flourished for several years in the discipline of business management. Business scholars study crowdsourcing mainly for its ability to generate revenue, reduce labor or production costs, and innovate new products and ideas for organizations. Understanding motivations and incentives for getting crowds to participate has been part of this line of research, too, as have numerous case studies of specific businesses that incorporate crowdsourcing or are based entirely on crowdsourcing.

Research related to crowdsourcing in computing and in business sometimes avoids the word *crowdsourcing*. For example, Luis von Ahn and Karim R. Lakhani, respected scholars who do crowdsourcing research in computing and business, respectively, prefer not to use the term *crowdsourcing* in their work. Von Ahn prefers *human computation*, a term he used long before *crowdsourcing* was coined, and Lakhani prefers *innovation* or *distributed innovation* because he sees the term *crowdsourcing* as conflating very different institutions and forms for eliciting labor and problem-solving skills. This resistance to the term *crowdsourcing* makes unified academic discourse about crowdsourcing challenging, and tying together these loose ends is one of the goals of this book.

Social science research focuses on the human dimension of crowdsourcing, which is concerned mostly with the who, why, and how of crowds. It examines the motivations for participation in crowdsourcing applications as well as the related issues of labor exploitation and ethics. Social science research on crowdsourcing also looks into the composition of crowds, with a focus on demographics and digital-divide issues, as well as questions of amateurism and professionalism. Interviews, case studies, and surveys are the most common methods employed in this line of research. Research into the motivations for participation by crowds is perhaps the most interdisciplinary thread of crowdsourcing research and is embraced by social scientists, business scholars, and computing researchers. Citations to papers on motivation tend to cross these disciplinary boundaries, but other theory building relating to crowdsourcing has difficulty jumping across disciplinary divides, probably due to deeper ontological and epistemological differences between the disciplines.

Various applied professional disciplines have focused on the application of crowdsourcing for specific industries and contexts, as well. These professional disciplines include urban planning, public administration, nursing and medicine, journalism, national security, and library science. Some of the research in this area is speculative and has proposed new applications for crowdsourcing in a given industry, while other research reports the results of actual cases of crowdsourcing in these contexts.

Managerial Commitments

In any crowdsourcing application, the organization needs to communicate to the crowd exactly how its ideas will affect the business of the organization going forward. Part of thinking about the organization of crowdsourcing applications involves determining levels of managerial commitment and execution. Organizations should make a commitment to use the crowd's input in a policy or an advisory capacity—or somewhere in between—before the launch of any crowdsourcing venture.

On the policy end of the policy-advisory spectrum, the organization launches a crowdsourcing application with the commitment to use the crowd's input in a direct, actionable way. The benefit of a government agency's embrace of a pure policy commitment is that members of the crowd know that they are being trusted with a serious public-participation activity, which may motivate them to participate in the crowdsourcing application. The disadvantage to this kind of policy commitment, however, is that if the organization is not pleased with the outcome of a crowdsourcing venture, it must backpedal and disappoint the crowd by reneging on the commitment to enact crowdsourced ideas.

On the advisory end of the policy-advisory spectrum, the organization makes no promises to members of the crowd to use any of their ideas. Rather, the organization states that the results of the crowdsourcing activity may or may not find their way into actual policy, production, or business operations. The advantage here is that the organization can solicit ideas from the crowd without having to commit to anything, but the disadvantage is that people may not participate if they do not feel that the organization will take their ideas seriously.

A point in the middle of the policy-advisory spectrum seems more reasonable for a crowdsourcing venture. In a peer-vetted creative-production crowdsourced design competition, for instance, the organization might commit to the top five-rated designs from the crowd but reserve the right to choose which of those five designs will be built. Or the organization might choose its top five designs and agree to build the one that gets the most votes. Another middle-of-the-road position is for the organization to appoint a panel of everyday citizens, organization representatives, and experts from a related profession to choose a winning design. A mix of these methods would have the crowd select the top five and a mixed panel of representatives select the winner. Whatever the level of commitment on the policy-advisory spectrum, the crowdsourcing organization needs to commit to the terms established at the outset of a crowdsourcing venture so that the crowd is not discouraged from participating in the organization's events in the future.

ISSUES IN CROWDSOURCING

Scholars have examined many facets of the crowdsourcing process, from how and why crowds participate in crowdsourcing applications to what ethical questions arise from crowdsourced labor and exploitation. Some of the most frequently mentioned scholarly issues and controversies surrounding crowdsourcing are addressed below.

Moving the Crowd

All individuals engaged in crowdsourcing are in some way motivated to participate, and understanding how and why crowds participate is necessary for designing effective crowdsourcing applications. The motivation to participate in crowdsourcing is not very different from the motivation to participate in blogging, creating open-source software, posting videos to YouTube, contributing to *Wikipedia*, or tagging content at Flickr.

Some common psychological dimensions of motivation provide a useful framework for this discussion. Edward L. Deci and Richard M. Ryan differentiate between intrinsic and extrinsic motivators in their self-determination theory. They write that "intrinsic motivation is defined as the doing of an activity for its inherent satisfactions rather than for some separable consequence" and that extrinsic motivation "pertains whenever an activity is done in order to attain some separable outcome."

When intrinsic motivators (such as fun or a challenge) and extrinsic motivators (such as financial reward, fame, or social pressure) interact, extrinsic rewards tend to undermine intrinsic motivation, and participants may engage in an activity for a variety of reasons both intrinsically and extrinsically motivated. For example, in a survey of the crowds at Taskcn.com, a Chinese crowdsourcing community, Haichao Zheng, Dahui Li, and Wenhua Hou found that intrinsic motivation was more important than extrinsic motivation in inducing participation on the site. In a study on Amazon Mechanical Turk, Jakob Rogstadius, Vassilis Kostakos, Aniket Kittur, Boris Smus, Jim Laredo, and Maja Vukovic found that intrinsic motivators generated a higher quality of work from crowds than extrinsic motivators did.

David Knoke and Christine Wright-Isak build on Deci and Ryan's intrinsic-extrinsic distinction by proposing three categories for understanding motivation—rational, norm-based, and affective. James L. Perry and Lois Recascino Wise summarize Knoke and Wright-Isak:

> Rational motives involve actions grounded in individual utility maximization. Norm-based motives refer to actions generated by efforts to conform to norms. Affective motives refer to triggers of behavior that are grounded in emotional responses to various social contexts.

Synthesizing Deci and Ryan's work with Knoke and Wright-Isak's work, we can view both the location of the motivator (intrinsic or from within as well as extrinsic or from outside) and the way that an internal need is fulfilled (rational, norm-based, or affective) as important for understanding the psychological dimensions of motivation.

Psychological motivational categories have been operationalized in many studies, in many contexts, and across many disciplines. In the communication and computing disciplines, a robust program of research has developed under the umbrella of uses and gratifications (U&G) theory and in the contexts of open-source software participation and the creation of user-generated content. U&G theory assumes an active audience that engages with various media while seeking certain gratifications. Since its maturation in the 1970s, U&G theory has evolved through hundreds of studies in communication and other disciplines.

Researchers in U&G studies catalog individuals' media use and media creation through self-reports in surveys and interviews and through observation and experimentation and develop extensive typologies explaining how and why individuals use media. This emphasis on descriptive typologies, rather than on coherent theory building and connection to psychological motivational categories, is one of the primary critiques of U&G theory. Nevertheless, U&G typologies serve an important purpose early in the development of any new media technology or technique because scholars must first catalog basic usage habits to understand the role that a technology plays in an individual's life and in society. This helps to set the stage for more sophisticated research and theory building later as technologies mature and their social impacts are easier to grasp. D. Harold Doty and William H. Glick made the case in a 1994 article for the theoretical usefulness of typologies generally, too.

Over the past decade, studies of motivations for open-source software and user-generated content production have illustrated such typologies. Henry Jenkins notes that members of any participatory culture "believe their contributions matter, and feel some degree of social connection with one another." Supporting this, Su-Houn Liu, Hsui-Li Liao, and Yuan-Tai Zeng found in a study of bloggers that "connecting with people" was the second most valued reward for blogging, behind the enjoyment of "pouring out feelings." For bloggers and other participants in social media arrangements, expressing themselves and having that expression met by others in the mediated space are what matter.

Some studies suggest that individuals in participatory cultures are more likely and motivated to contribute content to various social media sites when they perceive that peers are consuming and valuing their content. For instance, Michael J. Brzozowski, Thomas Sandholm, and Tad Hogg note that social media spaces within large enterprises sustain more participation when individuals in the space receive comments on their contributions to the commons and other indicators of peer value. Bernardo A. Huberman, Daniel M. Romero, and Fang Wu note a similar phenomenon regarding the motivations of YouTube members to post videos to the site and to continue posting videos over time. Fang Wu, Dennis M. Wilkinson, and Bernardo Huberman call these important processes of attention seeking and peer recognition "feedback loops." Individuals in participatory social media also find a kind of pure enjoyment in participating, as Oded Nov found in a survey of *Wikipedia* contributors, and individuals should have the opportunity to experience participation socially, with others, as Nov, Mor Naaman, and Chen Ye found in a study of content tagging at the photo-sharing site Flickr. Fun, connectedness, and peer feedback appear to be consistent motivators across several studies of participatory culture.

Several studies on motivation in open-source software participation support what open-source pioneer and founder of Linux, Linus Torvalds, predicted would be the primary motivator—the pleasure that is found in doing hobbies. As Torvalds stated in an interview with Rishab Aiyer Ghosh of the online journal *First Monday*, "most of the good programmers do programming not because they expect to get paid or get adulation by the public, but because it is *fun* to program." In fact, as Karim R. Lakhani and Robert G. Wolf point out, although much theorizing on individual motivation in open-source programming points to the primacy of extrinsic rewards (such as the opportunity for career advancement), intrinsic motivators (such as the enjoyment derived from building one's skills and solving tough coding problems) are more important. This emphasis on fun and self-fulfillment broadly resonates with many other motivational studies of social media.

All of this motivation research on digital phenomena applies to crowdsourcing. A number of interviews and surveys have been conducted at various crowdsourcing sites asking individuals in those crowds to explain why they participate. These studies show that people have many common reasons, both intrinsic and extrinsic, for participating but that no single motivator applies to all crowdsourcing applications. For instance, developing one's creative skills, building a portfolio for future employment, and challenging oneself to solve a difficult problem are motivators that emerge among several crowdsourcing cases, but some crowds are driven by financial gain and do not mention these intrinsic motivators.

Three quantitative surveys investigating the motivations of crowds paint a partial picture of how the rational, extrinsic opportunity to make money and other motivators drive the crowd's participation in crowdsourcing applications. In a study of the online community at iStockphoto.com, a stock photography and illustration crowdsourcing company, I found that the opportunity to earn money and the opportunity to develop one's creative skills trumped the desire to network with friends and other creative people and outranked other altruistic motivations. At crowdsourcing research and development company InnoCentive.com, Karim R. Lakhani, Lars Bo Jeppesen, Peter A. Lohse, and Jill A. Panetta found that intrinsic motivators (such as enjoying problem solving and cracking a tough problem) and financial rewards were significantly positively correlated to success as a solver on the site.

With the Finnish crowd-made film *Star Wreck: In the Pirkinning*, Katri Lietsala and Atte Joutsen found that the crowd participated in the creation of the movie because it was fun for passing time and they liked sharing knowledge and skills with others, among other altruistic reasons, but not because they wanted to make money. A series of online interviews that I conducted with the online community at Threadless.com, however, revealed that the primary motivators for participation were the opportunity to make money, develop creative skills, and find freelance work and a love for and addiction to the Threadless community.

Finally, in the crowdsourced transit-planning case Next Stop Design, career advancement, recognition by peers, contribution to a collaborative effort, self-expression, having fun, learning new skills, and low barriers to entry on the Web site all emerged as important motivators for participation.

These existing studies suggest that individuals who participate in crowdsourcing have the following motivations:

- to earn money,

- to develop creative skills,

- to network with other creative professionals,

- to build a portfolio for future employment,

- to challenge oneself to solve a tough problem,

- to socialize and make friends,

- to pass the time when bored,

- to contribute to a large project of common interest,

- to share with others, and

- to have fun.

The Myth about Amateur Crowds

Crowdsourcing has been linked with amateurism from the start. Jeff Howe's original 2006 article and its accompanying sidebar "Five Rules of the New Labor Pool" used the word *amateur* three times. And Howe launched a companion blog to his *Wired* article that was originally titled *Crowdsourcing: Tracking the Rise of the Amateur*, tethering the image of the amateur to the buzzword *crowdsourcing*. He later made a more sophisticated claim about amateurism in crowdsourcing in his book *Crowdsourcing: Why the Power of the Crowd Is Driving the Future of Business*. Howe argues in this book that individuals who participate in crowdsourcing applications are largely products of liberal arts educations, have many talents and creative interests, find themselves in the increasingly specialized work world of late capitalism, and seek crowdsourcing endeavors as a way to exercise their untapped talents. In the sense that their day jobs do not match their online creative pursuits, Howe calls these crowdsourcers amateurs.

The assumption that crowds are comprised of amateurs continues to permeate the popular press, but these assumptions do not appear to be coming true in anecdotal accounts or in the empirical research into crowdsourcing. Billy Federighi and Brett Snider were finalists in the 2007 Doritos Crash the Super Bowl ad contest, and their television commercial, "Mousetrap," aired during the

Super Bowl. When they created their ad, they were film students in Hollywood, with access to the training and equipment needed to make a professional-quality television package. They had already produced a television ad for Converse in 2006. Similarly, the Herbert brothers, who called themselves "two nobodies from nowhere" in a *USA Today* interview with Bruce Horovitz, were the winners of the 2009 Crash the Super Bowl contest. Despite the rags-to-riches rhetoric surrounding the jobless Herbert brothers, their winning entry, "Free Doritos," was made with the help of a crew of two dozen people, including media professionals.

iStockphoto and Threadless also seem ill-fitted to the amateur label. Despite being praised in Howe's original *Wired* article as a "marketplace for the work of amateur photographers—homemakers, students, engineers, dancers"—the crowdsourced, stock photography company iStockphoto seems largely a second market for professional stock photographers to sell their work. A 2007 survey of 651 iStockers found that 47 percent of participants felt that the term "professional" most accurately described them in terms of their creative talents (the most popular choice), with "hobbyist" the second most common (23 percent), and "amateur" the third most common (14 percent). Furthermore, 58 percent of iStockers surveyed had at least a year of formal schooling in art, design, photography, or a related creative discipline; more than one-fourth (26 percent) had more than five years of schooling; and 44 percent had more than five years of paid artistic experience.

Several of the winning designers at crowdsourced clothing company Threadless have been interviewed by members of the Threadless community, and these interviews are posted on Threadless's Web site. Many of these designers have won multiple Threadless contests, have their own robust freelance design portfolios, belong to organized design collectives, and work for graphic design, Web design, and advertising firms in creative roles. As noted in the discussion of motivations, interviews with Threadless community members found that the opportunity to make money and the potential to leverage Threadless participation for eventual freelance work were two of five primary motivators for participation on the Web site. Most of the winning Threadless designers do seem to be amateurs.

The crowdsourced scientific research and development company InnoCentive is also frequently cited as a place where "amateur scientists" or "garage scientists" can attempt tough chemical, engineering, or biological puzzles that have stymied major corporate lab staffs. It is a romantic but mistaken notion. Based on a survey of 320 participants in the InnoCentive "solver" community, Karim R. Lakhani and colleagues found that solvers were "highly qualified," with 65 percent of solvers holding doctorates and nearly 20 percent holding some other advanced degree, mostly degrees in the sciences. Finally, Next Stop Design was an attempt to test crowdsourcing in a public-participation context for transit planning, centered on a bus stop shelter design contest targeted at everyday bus riders. Interviews with twenty-three Next Stop Design participants revealed that the majority (eighteen) were either architects, intern architects seeking licensure, or architecture teachers. The nonarchitects included an electrical engineer, a surveyor, graphic designers, and a computer programmer, and many of these people mentioned that they had studied architecture in college.

The press has not been kind to the idea of amateur crowds, either. A 2012 analysis of news articles that mentioned the words *crowdsourcing* and *amateur* found that the press was especially distrustful, dismissive, and even condescending to amateur crowds. Headlines such as "Crowdsourcing starting to crowd out professionals" top articles describing armies of amateurs who are eager to dismantle the workings of entire professions. Some articles even describe crowds in condescending ways, referring to crowds as overly enthusiastic yet uninformed, and one article writes that professional work might be "difficult for the pajama-wearing amateur."

This unflattering coverage of crowdsourcing in the press reveals deeper anxieties about labor and the status of the creative professions. There is power in professionalization, and individuals who are seen as being outside of the boundaries of a profession are seen as not having access to that power. As George Ritzer wrote in 1975,

> [t]he single most important characteristic of the professions is seen as monopoly over their work tasks. A profession achieves such monopoly by convincing the state and the lay public that they need, and deserve, such a right. . . . We can see power as both the motor force behind drives toward professionalization as well as one of the defining characteristics of the professions.

In some ways, professionalism is a grab for power, a way to keep a wall between the sacred and the profane. Crowds and the low-cost, high-quality creative work they produce threaten the very notion of professionalism and the idea that knowledge and work opportunities should be restricted to the anointed few.

The research shows that crowds are decidedly more than just a collection of amateurs. They are a self-selecting group of experts and professionals with a keen interest in a given task, and this threatens professionalism. As Howe suggests in his book, participatory-culture arrangements like crowdsourcing call into question what defines an amateur or a professional in the first place.

Legal Issues

Because crowdsourcing blurs boundaries between professionalism and amateurism and between typical in-house business processes and external stakeholders, many legal issues surround the model. When governments employ crowdsourcing for public-participation programs, the preservation of free speech in crowdslapping cases is a concern. Issues of copyright and intellectual property are frequent concerns with crowdsourcing in business domains, and using crowdsourcing to assign microtasks to game social media sites or to plant favorable reviews for companies may count as deceptive business practices.

Free Speech and Dissent

Free societies defend the principle of free speech "not just because it is the law, but also because it is a really great idea," writes Lawrence Lessig in his book *Free Culture: How Big Media Uses Technology and the Law to Lock Down Culture and Control Creativity*: "A strongly protected tradition of free speech is likely to encourage a wide range of criticism. That criticism is likely, in turn, to improve the systems or people or ideas criticized." Free speech is a democratic value and also an important value within organizations for fostering innovation and problem solving, as Teresa Amabile and Eric von Hippel have each found. Surely free speech is crucial to the success of any crowdsourcing application, but what happens when crowds protest and threaten to destroy the application? This question is especially important for government-run crowdsourcing activities where the interests of the state and the citizenry intersect with good online community-management principles. A government-sponsored crowdsourcing application faces the challenge of managing citizens' protests without infringing on their right to speak about and against the government. This section explores some instances of crowd unrest, called *crowdslapping*, and methods for keeping crowdsourcing applications on track without censorship.

Various modes of crowd resistance include disruptive and destructive crowdslapping. In all cases, I favor regulating this speech by using the power of community norms and software code rather than overt forms of government censorship.

Disruptive crowdslapping resembles protest in physical public spaces. It seeks to disrupt the smooth operation of a crowdsourcing venture through complaints posted in online forums, criticisms of the government that do not stop others from being heard, and so on. This type of crowdslapping could take the form of a reasoned argument that is articulated by an individual in the crowd and posted to a crowdsourcing site, or it could take the form of a "peaceful" virtual petition against the government (or the specific government function under scrutiny in the crowdsourcing application).

Destructive crowdslapping, on the other hand, deters other citizens from participating on the site through aggressive attacks, such as *flaming*. John Suler, a researcher studying cyberpsychology, has studied an "online disinhibition effect" that results in "dissociative anonymity." He finds that "[w]hen people have the opportunity to separate their actions online from their in-person lifestyle and identity, they feel less vulnerable about self-disclosing and acting out." Flaming, or its cousin flooding, are tactics used by participants to lob insults (*flaming*) or cram an online bulletin board or chat space with junk text (*flooding*) as a way to decrease traffic to the site and destroy the potential for meaningful, rational online conversation. Indeed, the unruliness of some online crowds contrasts dramatically with the stilted visions of rational debate hoped for by online deliberative democracy's proponents. Still, from destructive flaming to disruptive criticism, these "slaps" from the crowd should be celebrated as moments of democratic engagement where even the most unpopular sentiments are valued as possible truths. That is what John Stuart Mill would want, at least.

Two other forms of crowd reaction, cracking and ignoring, can destroy a government crowdsourcing venture. *Cracking*, the accurate term for malicious hacking, is taking action to destroy the mechanisms of the site, probably through unlawful access to and manipulation of the site's code. Destructive crowdslapping deters productive dialog in a crowdsourcing application, but cracking prevents individuals from engaging with the crowdsourcing project. This involves shutting down chat and bulletin board spaces, corrupting data files, and otherwise breaking the site. When this form of malicious activity occurs on a crowdsourcing site, a government crowdsourcer should take action to stop it because it threatens a public forum and prevents people from engaging in self-governance.

The final form of crowd resistance, *ignoring*, is the most peaceful and probably the most effective. Crowdsourcing ventures require a sizable crowd of individuals who each try to solve a given problem. Without enough minds tackling the problem, the process fails. In a 2003 law journal article, Beth Simone Noveck examined online government ventures that were struggling to attract a critical mass of users.

These four forms of crowd resistance (disruptive crowdslapping, destructive crowdslapping, cracking, and ignoring) are akin to traditional methods of protest—respectively, lobbying and rational debate, annoying chants and image events, destruction of a public forum through a bomb threat, and boycotting.

In the United States, public-participation activities are a matter of public record, and online public-participation activities, such as government crowdsourcing applications, occupy a complicated place legally. It is not surprising that outdated metaphors and ways of understanding the law have caused the law to lag behind the pace of technology, and in the case of speech in online public-participation applications, the concept of the physical forum comes into play. In US law, there are three different kinds of forums—the traditional forum, the limited public forum, and the nonpublic forum. Streets and parks, where citizens enjoy the widest free speech rights, are examples of traditional public forums. Public meetings at city council are examples of limited public forums, where government can control the topics and time allotted to speakers. Nonpublic forums, such as jails and schools, are spaces where government has the greatest control over speech. Generally, in limited public forums, governments may control the time, place, and manner (for example, prohibiting profanity) of speech in content-neutral ways for the sake of civil discourse, while in nonpublic forums governments may censor speech based on content as well.

A government crowdsourcing application may be considered more like a traditional public-participation activity, such as a workshop or hearing, and thus is more like a limited public forum in legal terms. If a crowdsourcing application uses third-party platforms, such as Facebook or Twitter, the terms of use for those sites, which include provisions against threatening and hateful content, govern the application. Administrators may also impose restrictions on discussion topics beyond the narrow scope of a crowdsourcing project; however, "it may be difficult . . .

to reap the benefits of public participation in social media if there are too many limitations on what may be posted," writes Frayda Bluestein on the *Coates' Canons* blog. At a certain point, too many government restrictions on speech may turn participants away from a crowdsourcing project, which could cause the project to collapse for lack of input or interest.

I believe that governments should impose only minimal restrictions on speech in crowdsourcing applications and instead should empower the crowd with the tools—code—necessary to self-govern through community standards.

In his book *Constitutional Domains: Democracy, Community, Management*, Robert C. Post makes the case for community standards as an effective way to resolve legal disputes, noting that communities have a good understanding of what is effective and appropriate for themselves. Applied online, the heuristic of community norms and standards is evident in some of the most robust, long-lasting communities. In these successful online communities, newcomers are treated with caution, and the established communities work collectively to ignore or engage dissent from outsiders productively in ways that protect the values of the community. As Lawrence Lessig has pointed out, however, this vision of community policing only goes so far. Without technological prevention tools, for instance, outsiders may insert themselves into an online community forum and rant excessively. Existing community members may ignore or productively engage outsiders, but they can do little to stop their annoying posts. If the outsider is persistent enough, existing community members will grow tired of the rants and will exit the community, which may lead to the community's ultimate collapse.

Thus, the most effective online communities are equipped with lines of software code that enable the community to deal effectively with others and help to enforce community standards. For example, a simple code-based regulation in an online forum might limit message length or prevent someone from posting the same message multiple times in a row (for example, posting spam advertising in chat rooms). Online communities can establish constitutions that empower the most senior members to block users who violate those terms, although this is a problematic solution because the power to censor is merely shifted from government to a select few citizens, and this also departs from the ideal of the marketplace of ideas. Alternatively, communities may vote to suppress— but not entirely delete—some postings to the bottom of the heap or discussion thread. Still other code-based tools enable communities to assign reputational rankings to their peers, providing a kind of shorthand clue (usually through an icon) to others testifying to the quality of that member's comments. On eBay, reputation icons serve this function. As eBay buyers and sellers amass more success-ful transactions and provide good customer service to each other, members have the opportunity to leave feedback for each other and affect each other's reputation and status as trusted buyers and sellers. Lessig argues that this kind of information architecture through software code technology empowers communities to live out their desires to self-govern through community norms.

A crowdsourcing application with the right software tools generally can empower citizens to regulate themselves. And when citizens threaten to destroy civil dialog, governments have the ability to restrict speech in the spirit of the limited public forum.

Intellectual Property and Copyright

Any Web site, but especially one that features user-generated content, needs to have in place terms of use, Digital Millennium Copyright Act (DMCA) statements, and other policies that protect both the crowdsourcing organization and the crowd. The most successful crowdsourcing companies have policies in place to protect both parties fairly, and these policies are easy to find and understand. InnoCentive, for example, states in plain language how intellectual property is handled on the site. Individuals in the crowd who attempt to solve challenges posted by Seeker companies sign a legal agreement to protect confidential information, and a decision to submit a possible solution to a challenge is an agreement to grant the Seeker company a temporary ninety-day exclusive license to the intellectual property in a submission. For InnoCentive's theoretical and reduction-to-practice challenges, Seeker companies take full ownership of intellectual property when full awards are paid. When only a partial award is offered by a Seeker company for part of a solution, the Solver has the ability to reject the offer and retain intellectual property rights over his or her submission. As the locus of control in crowdsourcing is situated in a shared space between organization and crowd, such a policy offers a measure of protection for both the organization and the crowd as part of the work arrangement.

Threadless has a similar straightforward policy regarding intellectual property that is fair to both the company and the crowd. After a member of the Threadless community submits a design to the Threadless site, he or she essentially grants Threadless temporary commercial rights for ninety days, and any design that Threadless prints will result in the stated prize money paid to the community member. If the submission is not selected for printing, the community member retains the intellectual property rights over his or her design. It is a simple and fair agreement, but not all crowdsourcing applications set out with these intentions. An industrial design crowdsourcing competition in 2011 failed in part because the organization insisted on retaining all intellectual property rights to all submissions, even those that did not win the competition. In response to these policies, some designers told the crowdsourcing project manager that they were unwilling to participate because the contest represented a "work on spec" arrangement, which more and more creative professionals are resisting. Spec work is discussed in greater detail in this chapter's section on ethics.

Crowdsourcing organizations must also remain vigilant against potential copyright violations of third-party content that is submitted to crowdsourcing competitions. Although all successful crowdsourcing businesses have rules that prohibit users from submitting content that belongs to another party, the organization needs to ensure that any idea or product from the crowd that it puts into production is truly an original creation of an individual in the crowd. Mistakenly manufacturing another person's design submitted by the crowd could involve the crowdsourcing organization in complex and undesirable legal settlements. One example of such a legal situation is crowdfunding company Kickstarter's November 2012 lawsuit involving a 3D printer project it funded on its site. According to a BBC report, US technology company Formlabs solicited more than $2.9 million from more than 2,000 users on Kickstarter to produce a 3D printer, but 3D printing company 3D Systems has filed suit against Formlabs claiming Formlabs' Kickstarter project incorporated one of 3D Systems' patents without permission. The lawsuit is pending at the time of this book's publication.

Unfair Business Practices

Most new business models have negative aspects, and all markets have black markets. Crowdsourcing is no exception, and the distributed-human-intelligence tasking form of crowdsourcing enables a specific form of market manipulation that could be cause for legal concern. In a provocative 2011 article for the *Hastings Science and Technology Law Journal*, Peter Touschner argued that online social media black markets, specifically the crowdsourcing company Subvert and Profit, violate part of the US Federal Trade Commission (FTC) Act. The FTC regulates unfair and monopolistic business practices and has noted that the rise of consumer-created content published online presents unique challenges to the agency. One challenge is that individuals who write opinions and reviews of products online become, in the eyes of others online, trusted sources for information about those businesses. Section 5 of the FTC Act is the FTC's Policy Statement on Deception. Touschner argues that "Section 5 is broad enough and flexible enough to encompass such 'black markets' in its definition of 'unfair or deceptive acts or practices in or affecting commerce.'" Because microtask Web sites like Subvert and Profit traffic in paid false endorsements of products, services, and Web sites, they enable a level of deception that interferes in fair, competitive business practice.

The information technology research and advisory company Gartner estimates that fully 10 to 15 percent of social media reviews will be fake by 2014. These reviews will be purchased by companies as part of regular, covert advertising buys. Gartner also predicts that at least two Fortune 500 companies will face FTC litigation in the coming few years over this practice.

Ethical Issues

Charges of "click servitude," "digital slavery," and "crowdsploitation" have been lodged against crowdsourcing operations by critics. On the surface, crowdsourcing is an easy path to fast, cheap, high-quality labor. Crowdsourcing organizations benefit from the work of crowds without offering the kinds of monetary rewards that are the norm in traditional work arrangements. Some claim that crowds undercut the professional class, undoing years of advocacy by professional associations to boost pay rates, protect workers, and establish ethical standards for professional work. The question of labor exploitation in crowds is complex, however. So-called digital sweatshops are not the same as actual offline sweatshops in many regards, as crowds work voluntarily in crowdsourcing arrangements. Additionally, crowdsourcing is not always an efficient model for the organization.

Labor Rights

Discussions of amateurism in the popular press's coverage of crowdsourcing may serve as a red herring to divert attention away from the fact that many professionals were struggling to make a living before crowdsourcing's arrival. On Jeff Howe's crowdsourcing blog, professional photographer Russell Kord ranted about iStockphoto's negative effect on his business: "digital cameras have taken away the skill necessary to expose a decent image, composition is a matter of opinion, and distribution is now cheap and easy." In the wake of crowdsourcing, professionals operating in the old paradigm of creative production are affected, but creative professionals were not at the top of the income ladder before crowdsourcing. The popular crowdsourcing coverage scapegoats amateurs as the reason that artists suffer, and journalists covering crowdsourcing emphasize the "lowly paid amateur's" willingness to work for as little as "$1 to $5," to work "inexpensively," or to work "for free." These articles frame this low-cost amateur labor as good for business, allowing greater profit margins and less wasteful spending on in-house scientists or in-house creative professionals. Ultimately, the discourse of amateurism in crowdsourcing falsely positions amateurs—who often are as qualified and committed as professionals—as the barbarians at the gate, disrupting the tidy status quo of enterprise. This discourse blames crowdsourcing and amateurs as outside forces that drive down industry prices, even though a race to the bottom was already happening in the creative industries.

Some journalists adopt sympathetic stances toward the crowd (yet still refer to them as amateurs), and they express concern for the exploitive potential of crowdsourcing arrangements. Some pay rates are extremely low in paid crowdsourcing applications. At Mechanical Turk, many of the most active Turkers average only $2 per hour, and according to a 2010 survey by Panagiotis G. Ipeirotis, many of these workers are highly educated and come from industrialized nations, with about half coming from the United States. In any other work arrangement, these circumstances would lead anyone to question the fairness of crowdsourcing.

This leads to the question of whether exploited crowds can organize against unfair labor practices. Because crowds are positioned in the discourse as groups of amateurs and hobbyists to whom organizations outsource tasks, they are discursively denied the opportunity to organize in the way professionals would. There are no unions, no professional ethical codes, no official associations to define standards, and no formal arrangement for individuals in the crowd to discuss equity in pay or intellectual property rights over their ideas. The apparatus of professionalism, however, provides these safeguards, exerting authority and prestige and autonomy to protect and serve members of the profession. The amateur label portrays the crowd as a nonprofessional, never-professional horde, a group that cannot and should not organize for its own good. Distributed labor, whether outsourced overseas or crowdsourced over the Internet, is a hallmark of global capitalism and a proven strategy for deflating the power of unions and hindering labor organizing. As I have argued, crowds are largely professional, not amateur, yet lack the basic apparatus of professionalism to protect them as workers, and the popular discourse about their amateur status keeps this apparatus at bay.

There is perhaps one consolation for crowds in terms of organizing. Any crowdsourcing application is only as vibrant as its online community. A crowd dissatisfied with a crowdsourcing organization is free to leave, and a large enough exodus can cause a crowdsourcing application to collapse entirely. Although rare, crowds can resist within the crowdsourcing apparatus and implement a range of tactics, including disruptive crowdslapping, destructive crowdslapping, and malicious hacking. Unfortunately, though, organizations can make Web site architecture choices (such as not including a discussion forum) and policy choices (such as imposing restrictions on terms of use) to inhibit this crowd organizing within the crowdsourcing application. Given the ability of crowds to leave at any time, it is difficult to call crowdsourcing exploitive.

If professionalism is what Valérie Fournier calls "one of the new softwares of control" that disciplines workers

Any crowdsourcing application is only as vibrant as its online community. A crowd dissatisfied with a crowdsourcing organization is free to leave, and a large enough exodus can cause a crowdsourcing application to collapse entirely.

in late capitalist economies, then celebrating the amateur in crowdsourcing as a counterpoint to the professional obscures the fact that these amateurs uphold capitalist systems through their work, too. In his book *Convergence Culture: Where Old and New Media Collide*, Henry Jenkins reminds us that "the emergent knowledge culture will never fully escape the influence of commodity culture, any more than commodity culture can totally function outside the constraints of the nation-state." Any individual in the crowd, whether amateur or professional, who engages in a for-profit crowdsourcing application accepts his or her position within a capitalist enterprise. It is an illusion that the crowd controls the products they produce or the means of production through their submissions to a crowdsourcing site. They are laborers, not owners, and "amateur" laborers accept an even lower status in that arrangement than "professionals." Yet the label of amateur conjures an impression that what really takes place on a crowdsourcing Web site is democratic.

The word *democratization* appears in both the popular and scholarly discourse on crowdsourcing. Crowdsourcing is discursively aligned with open innovation practices, and Eric von Hippel's book on the topic, *Democratizing Innovation*, embraces the term. But democratization is also a common buzzword uncritically associated with all things Web 2.0, especially concerning Web 2.0 business practices. In a critical analysis of Web 2.0 business manifestos, José

Van Dijck and David Nieborg argue that "in marketing and business discourse, cultural terms such as 'communities' and 'collaboration' are rapidly replacing economic terms such as 'consumers,' 'commodities,' and 'customization.'" This problematic conflation of commons with commerce permits companies to shift the "locus of value extraction" to users, strip-mine consumers for value, and celebrate it as "co-creation."

Amateurs are everyday people like us, and "democratized" crowdsourcing applications allow us to feel as though we are part of something big and collective, as if we are cocreating a bold new future alongside hip companies. If something is made "by us and for us," carrying the hollow label of democracy, then we feel it is automatically better, was not expertly targeted to us by profit-hungry companies, and was not spun by politically biased news organizations (in the case of crowdsourced journalism). This discourse of amateurism makes us feel more empowered and more in control of the products and media that we consume. But these so-called amateurs are really outsourced professionals, and the products and media content that we are sold are not much different from the old products. They certainly are no more democratically created and never beyond the grip of capitalist logic.

In the end, companies never lose with crowdsourcing, and it could be argued that members of crowds, who work willingly, never truly lose either. Because the locus of value extraction shifts to the amateur consumer-creator and away from the product, all failures can be pinned on the backs of the crowd. This is fail-safe public relations for crowdsourcing organizations. Some journalists discuss the benefits of letting the amateur crowd attempt a project even though the quality might be low because the crowd will have ordered sloppy work for itself. As a June 2011 *New York Times* article put it, "amateurs . . . challenge our notion of quality." The discourse of amateurism is problematic because it allows companies to outsource responsibility to the crowd. If a company can claim it opened itself to input from the crowd, then it can similarly avoid accountability for crowdsourced media content that flops in the television ratings, products that do not sell, media content that perpetuates stereotypes, and other failures. In the face of a crowd-made failure, a company can win with public relations, claiming that it engaged consumers with the brand more intimately than it ever had before. It can embrace the Web 2.0 values of transparency and openness and tell the crowd that it got what it wanted. And in the face of failure, companies can always use the experience to justify leaving crowdsourcing behind and hiring professional talent the old-fashioned way.

Efficient for Whom?

Cheap as crowdsourcing may be for organizations, it may not be efficient in the wider view. With a company like

InnoCentive, for example, the crowd consists largely of professionally trained scientists with graduate degrees. In a given challenge, dozens of scientists may spend time attempting to solve a tough problem. A few of those scientists will submit solutions. All this problem solving, especially for those who submit solutions, consumes a large amount of time. Winning solutions at InnoCentive are rewarded with handsome prizes, but the prizes are still far cheaper than what it would normally cost an organization to run an in-house lab. It is an efficiency "win" for the crowdsourcer at InnoCentive, but it can be seen as an overall loss in terms of scientific intellect. Many hours' worth of professional scientific training are wasted in the system, and it raises the question of what else that scientific talent could have been doing. What other problems were *not* solved? Seen through this lens, then, crowdsourcing may be an inefficient model for solving tough problems, and this is an argument for the use of traditional models as a supplement to crowdsourcing.

Creative professionals put together polished designs or other samples to attract business as part of a portfolio. Some work as freelancers, and others will work "on spec," or speculatively, to perform work without the guarantee of payment in hopes of securing future paid work. There is considerable backlash against the practice of speculative work among creative workers. The NO!SPEC Web site warns that "spec work and spec-based design contests are a growing concern," and the site's organizers ask for international support in "promoting professional, ethical business practices by saying NO! to spec." Crowdsourced design contests on reputable sites, such as Threadless, guarantee fair treatment of designers through legal terms and attractive case prizes. But newcomers to crowdsourcing may not think about the ethics of demanding professional designers to submit work on spec without the guarantee of intellectual property rights or fair pay. According to interviews with Threadless designers in 2010, some are wary of posting even half-baked ideas on the site for fear that others in the community might borrow from them too heavily without proper attribution. The distinction between amateur and professional, then, may be better explained as a continuum of work relationships between individual and organization. Those permanently employed by an organization may long for greater autonomy, and those temporarily employed by an organization (for example, in freelance arrangements) may hope for better job security. All of this complicates the amateur or professional or pro-am identity of today's media worker. And the prevalence of spec work further muddies these boundaries, luring aspiring designers to crowdsourced design contests to the detriment of established professional designers who have fought hard to ensure fair pay upfront for professional creative services.

Strategic Communication and Social Media Gaming

Some uses for crowdsourcing can be seen as sinister or manipulative. Strategic communication professionals must decide whether tools like Subvert and Profit are ethical because they run counter to many of the tenets of ethical strategic communication practice. Ideally, strategic communication professionals—an umbrella term that includes public relations, marketing, advertising, and related professionals—are bound by prescriptive professional ethical codes in their work. The most widely known strategic communication ethical codes are those of the Public Relations Society of America (PRSA) and the International Association of Business Communicators (IABC). Most university public relations curricula in the United States also require courses in ethics and emphasize the tenets of these codes for undergraduate majors. Essentially, then, professional codes of ethics are considered part of the core of good strategic communication practice.

But in many ways, the principles of the PRSA and IABC ethical codes run counter to the nature of Subvert and Profit. Subvert and Profit violates these codes by restricting the free flow of information, not serving the public interest, not making honest disclosures, and violating principles of honesty, fairness, advocacy, and loyalty. Some strategic communication bloggers have criticized Subvert and Profit for not being as effective as it claims to be, but there is a lack of discussion about the ethical implications of using a service like Subvert and Profit in the first place.

At a time when strategic communication professionals blindly turn to technologies that appear to be effective in making something "go viral" online, it is important to consider the ethical practices of online community and social media management, which are emerging strategic communication professions in today's landscape. To remain compliant with PRSA and IABC ethical codes, strategic communication professionals need to consider the relationships and implications of the crowdsourcing model rather than see it uncritically as just another tool in the social media tool bag.

Aesthetic Tyranny

Although Internet penetration is now high in industrialized nations and is rapidly growing in developing countries, many digital divides prevent crowds from being maximally diverse and universally accessible. In the United States, for example, many rural areas are still without broadband connections, and African Americans and Spanish-speaking Latinos are among the least connected demographically. Since crowdsourcing is necessarily an online phenomenon and not everyone has access to the Internet, no crowdsourcing application is accessible to all. Yet claims of democracy and "of the people, by the people" surround crowdsourcing.

When a crowd is not maximally inclusive, it may not perform as well as it might have if it were more diverse. In addition, a kind of aesthetic tyranny is possible in crowdsourced design competitions, and a crowdsourced policy project may result in a policy that fails to serve some of its stakeholders. If crowds are relatively homogeneous and elite in their makeup, then crowdsourcing applications may reproduce the hegemonic values of those in power through creative production. This is especially problematic when the process is glossed over as "democratic."

In crowdsourced public-participation programs for governance, this kind of exclusion means that the voices of the marginalized are not heard because the people who are underrepresented in traditional public-participation programs are also the same people who are likely to be without an Internet connection. Crowdsourced public-participation programs for governance or planning should thus supplement rather than supplant traditional public-participation activities.

THE FUTURE OF CROWDSOURCING

Crowdsourcing has steadily proliferated across many disciplines and into new contexts as new industries embrace the model to rejigger old and inefficient operations and to invent entirely new uses. Where crowdsourcing goes, researchers follow. In this chapter, I outline future growth areas for crowdsourcing, both in new applications and new research directions across disciplines.

Future Technology

As ubiquitous computing becomes the norm in our lives, flexible crowdsourcing platforms will become easy for everyday people to use and will be seamlessly integrated into our normal life processes. The success of platforms like InnoCentive and Mechanical Turk demonstrates the usefulness of easy-to-use platforms that individuals and organizations can access for specific problem-solving purposes on an as-needed basis. Wide-reaching, flexible platforms will come to predominate over in-house and ad-hoc crowdsourcing applications. This presents opportunities for organizations that do not need or cannot afford to set up their own large-scale crowdsourcing applications. Crowdsourcing platforms will come to be seen by organizations as run-of-the-mill third-party vendors, not much different from copying and printing vendors, shipping and logistics vendors, or management consultants.

In this sense, the question of technology for organizations will be moot. Crowdsourcing will move from a technological approach to a business service. IT advisory services, such as Gartner and Forrester, or management consulting firms, such as McKinsey or Boston Consulting Group, will eventually rate crowdsourcing platforms and advise on their strategic use, and key officers in an organization will make the decisions about which crowdsourcing platforms to engage. The technology that drives crowdsourcing is relatively simple. Most crowdsourcing applications are similar to basic mobile applications or Web sites that run on content-management systems. Crowdsourcing is a process for connecting organizations to online communities and exchanging information between them. Free, open-source code for crowdsourcing applications is available now, and eventually the technological skeleton of crowdsourcing will be as widely taken for granted by

Crowdsourcing platforms will come to be seen by organizations as run-of-the-mill third-party vendors, not much different from copying and printing vendors, shipping and logistics vendors, or management consultants.

organizations and users as the technological skeleton of email.

There will also be a general trend toward the increasing use of crowdsourcing platforms that use mobile technology. Mobile phones are bridging the digital divide in developing nations around the world as more people access the Internet via mobile devices than via laptops or desktop computers. Crowdsourcing applications will adapt to allow SMS-based contributions as well as rich mobile Web contributions from smart phones. Flexible crowdsourcing platforms that automatically reconfigure for mobile browsing will be optimal. Ushahidi and other crowdsourcing services that have taken hold in developing countries demonstrate the potential for growth in crowdsourcing around the world, enabled by widespread mobile phone use.

Future Applications

As an application of deliberative democratic theory, traditional public-participation programs in urban planning and governance seek to cultivate citizen input and produce public decisions that are agreeable to all stakeholders. In one public-participation context, involving citizens in the urban-planning process helps ensure that a plan will be more widely accepted by its future users.

Public-participation programs in urban planning also value nonexpert or nonmainstream knowledge brought into the creative problem-solving process of planning. In the past three years, many US government offices have started crowdsourcing initiatives or contests to reimagine operations or incentivize innovative applications of public policy. In the future, democratic governance will regularly include crowdsourcing. Eventually, public input will be gathered in nearly every facet of governance, and crowdsourcing applications will enable this process. Crowdsourcing applications in governance will focus on improving transparency and efficiency in the near future, and eventually, large-scale peer-vetted creative-production applications will appear in a variety of governmental contexts.

The Peer-to-Patent project will be a permanent fixture in patent-application review at the US Patent and Trademark Office. The US Geological Survey continues to make use of the "Did You Feel It?" Web site that allows citizens to report earthquake tremors to an online map, much like Ushahidi. And the US Office of Management and Budget's SAVE Award will continue to solicit government employees' cost-cutting ideas. Future government applications of crowdsourcing might include using the knowledge-discovery and -management approach to report public transit use, to catalog public art projects and murals, or to report disrepair or sightings of dangerous animals in national parks. Broadcast search applications might include identifying better algorithms for timing traffic signals or improving actuarial formulas and behavioral modeling for social security or health insurance programs. Peer-vetted creative-production approaches for governance could expand to include the planning and design of large-scale urban development or public art projects, the crafting of public policy, and school redistricting and busing plans. And distributed-human-intelligence tasking for governance could include historical document analysis, language translation for government Web sites and documents, and the crowdsourcing of all kinds of data entry.

In the area of national security, crowdsourcing has already become a top priority. The US Defense Advanced Research Projects Agency (DARPA) has incorporated crowdsourcing into some of its focus areas, hoping to develop new systems for improving operations by tapping collective intelligence among soldiers in combat, topical experts across the country, and diplomatic officers overseas. DARPA's flirtation with crowdsourcing was best illustrated by the 2009 DARPA Network Challenge, also referred to as the DARPA Red Balloon Challenge. To test the speed and accuracy of distributed reporting around the globe, DARPA offered a cash prize to individuals who located big red balloons placed in undisclosed locations around the United States.

Some other national security goals that might be met with crowdsourcing include preempting terrorism, reducing casualties in battle, and better assessing threats to critical computer systems. The US Air Force and other defense and security offices have also explored crowdsourcing. The use of crowds, even if the crowds are limited to individuals with certain levels of security clearance, will become commonplace in defense and security industries and agencies. The number of calls for proposals being issued by the Department of Defense that mention crowdsourcing indicates that crowdsourcing is going to expand in national security applications.

Crowdsourcing has been tested in the field of journalism but with only modest success. Using crowds is not the best way to write entire stories collaboratively, as Assignment Zero proved, but crowds may be useful in one of the four problem types suitable for crowdsourcing. The future of journalism will involve crowds in crunching big data, fact checking, copy editing, information gathering, and contributing to rich investigative reports that may restore the press as the fourth estate in US governance. Flexible all-purpose crowdsourcing platforms will become the norm in large news organizations, in part due to shrinking budgets in news organizations. An entire class of professional-amateur journalists will form crowds that will engage in these important news functions.

Crowdsourcing will continue to affect the science and health fields, taking cues from the success of crowdsourcing applications such as InnoCentive. Larger slices of corporate research and development work will become entrusted to the crowd. More complicated intellectual property arrangements may emerge from the increased number of applications of crowdsourcing for science and engineering. And in the domain of health, crowdsourcing will be deployed to accelerate and improve public health interventions, such as reporting violations in point-of-sale tobacco control. Crowdsourcing will also prove useful in gathering health histories, using human computation to transcribe older health records, and developing sophisticated models to improve health behavior.

Crowdsourcing has already been proven to be effective in language translation, and this application of the model will become more common. The model will also be used in the learning of foreign languages. Luis von Ahn, for example, has applied the principles of his reCAPTCHA system to a new language teaching system called Duolingo. Using crowdsourcing to teach people new languages easily and cheaply and to translate more of the world's information into different languages will help spread research, news, and public health information globally.

Future Research Directions

Future research on crowdsourcing will continue to focus on motivations for participation. These studies will refine existing motivational typologies and begin to determine which motivators are most important in specific crowdsourcing types. Although we know much about the many reasons crowds participate and we know there are multiple kinds of participants in each crowdsourcing application, we are as yet unclear as to which motivators are more important than others, whether some motivators are more prominent in certain crowdsourcing types, and whether different kinds of crowds or personality types predict certain primary motivators for participation. Empirical data to answer these questions are needed to design future crowdsourcing applications.

Research into the performance of crowdsourcing systems is still needed, especially as industries morph the crowdsourcing model to address new problems. These studies attempt to understand the conditions that produce the most productive outcomes in crowdsourcing. To date, business and computing scholars have been the primary voices in research on the performance of crowdsourcing systems. As crowdsourcing grows in new disciplines, scholars in those new disciplines need to assess and experiment with crowdsourcing to improve its function. Crowdsourcing is a problem-solving model and requires constant tweaks to achieve optimal performance. Ideally, there will be interdisciplinary collaborations between the scholars in these disciplines and the performance research scholars in business and computing.

As mobile platforms become more common in crowdsourcing, research will be needed to figure out how best to maximize the benefits of place-based data in crowdsourcing. Participatory geographic information system studies are underway to discover how people provide useful geographic data to central systems in a crowdsourced fashion. Mobile phones carried around a city by willing participants can passively report real-time data about any number of issues in real space. Studies in this vein should consider the performance and motivations of participants and also imagine new applications and new problems that can be solved with the advantage of mobile computational power. Larger questions of how citizens engage with government and with public space, from a cultural perspective, are also pertinent here.

Lastly, as the term *big data* becomes a buzzword in many circles, ways to process those data will be needed. Crowdsourcing seems a natural approach, especially for data that require human intelligence to process. Research into crowdsourced data analysis could include performance studies and case-study syntheses. Research in the spirit of Bongard and colleagues' work on crowdsourced variables for behavioral modeling would also help us tackle data problems that were once considered too large or complex to address with computers alone.

Research into the Online Community-Management Profession

New technologies make new economies, and new economies make new jobs. I predict that we will see many new jobs that fall under the umbrella of online community management in the coming years, and research will be needed to make sense of these new professions. Strategic communication offers a unique insight into this new work. Relationships between an organization and its stakeholders (customers, clients, donors, employees) are usually strongest when they are mutually beneficial, when they are symmetrical and communication flows two ways, and when they are at the core of strategic-communication practice.

Strategic communication involves investing in the process of maintaining relationships with stakeholders to achieve management goals. Because many companies and nonprofits (and even government functions) rely on the maintenance of healthy, productive, and sometimes sizeable online communities, strategic communication is an apt framework for understanding how organizations can maintain relationships with these communities.

Some research in this vein will focus on best practices and policies for online community management. Ansgar Zerfass, Stephan Fink, and Anne Linke found that many companies lack sufficient social media governance frameworks, including a lack of social media policies, social media staffing, budgets, strategy papers, and assessment standards. The same is presumably true of online community management, and research will be needed to craft good online community-governance policies for organizations looking to crowdsource. Research into how and why communities form and are sustained is necessary as well. Much of this is connected to motivation research.

Some key questions about the emerging profession of online community management will require further study, and I organize these key questions under broad pursuits of knowledge about stakeholders, growth, motivations, success, and professionalism.

Understanding exactly who participates in crowdsourcing projects is important because different types of people have different capabilities, talents, and motivations. Some crowdsourcing projects require stakeholders that are demographically or cognitively diverse to succeed, and some projects, such as collaborative policymaking projects or urban-planning projects, seek stakeholder groups that have investments in a jurisdiction. Research projects should focus on identifying who participates in an online community, what their talents and perspectives are, and how desired stakeholders can be recruited into a crowdsourcing project's online community. More important, though, research is needed to understand the needs and expectations of these online communities so that strategic-communication practitioners, serving perhaps in online community-manager roles, are able to foster relationships between the organization and its stakeholders. If relationship maintenance is a key to good strategic-communication practice, then figuring out who will participate in these relationships is paramount.

A scientific understanding of how online communities form, how they grow, and how they decline is desperately needed. The question of how many people are needed to make a group collectively intelligent is important, but an equally important question is how to ensure those numbers are achieved and sustained. If an online community is slow to get started, new visitors will see it as a ghost town and may turn away, preventing an online community from growing to the critical mass that it needs to function as an intelligent collective. Likewise, large, already established online communities may repel newcomers, who may be intimidated by an exclusive community with its own norms. Studies into the effectiveness of strategic-communication tactics that are used to recruit and retain online communities would be useful here.

There is a robust body of research into the motivations of individuals who participate in online communities. This line of work ought to continue with collective-intelligence projects, focusing on why participants are drawn to online communities and what they seek in a relationship with an organization.

A strategic-communication perspective can contribute to the study of whether and how crowdsourcing projects succeed by focusing on the online community's perceptions of the project as a whole. Strategic-communication practitioners routinely assess branding success and other perceptions among stakeholders, and strategies are adjusted accordingly. Crowdsourcing research that is too focused on system performance and technical achievement may miss this crucial human point. Research into crowdsourcing project success should consider the project appraisals and perceptions of online community members as serious factors in the overall success of a system. For instance, a crowdsourcing project that is focused on public participation in urban planning would need to ask participants about their perceptions of the project according to established principles of good online public-deliberation design.

New positions within strategic communication are already being developed. Strategic-communication job boards are listing job titles such as online community managers, social media managers, online customer-care specialists, and Twitter managers. As with any segment of strategic communication or any professional practice, there is a concern for developing best practices and building professional standards and ethical guidelines. This work should continue in the direction of crowdsourcing projects, centered on the work of those who strategically manage the projects and their online communities.

Studying online communities is complex work. It is humanistic and social scientific and is often interdisciplinary in its orientation. Interdisciplinary teams of researchers could contribute greatly to our understanding of how crowdsourcing projects and online communities are managed. Furthermore, there is room for both qualitative and quantitative methods in the study of online communities, with quantitative studies producing results that can be generalized and qualitative studies uncovering the richness of individual experiences or discrete cases. Holistic case-study research, a common approach in strategic-communication scholarship, would also be appropriate.

As the field of crowdsourcing grows, so too does the need for an understanding of the practical management of such projects and communities. Strategic communication offers a useful lens for viewing this research because it brings the practice of strategic-communication campaign planning to bear on this work. As we learn more about how crowdsourcing works, we may also learn how best to make it work effectively, ultimately putting this knowledge to work to improve the world through social, environmental, and democratic projects for the public good.

Research into the Professional Crowd
If online community management is a useful way to think about the professionalization of crowdsourcing from the organization's standpoint, then what is the perspective of professionalization from the crowd's standpoint? Will we begin to see individuals who consider themselves full-time members of crowds and who make a living through participation in one or multiple crowdsourcing platforms? In some cases, this is already happening.

Panagiotis Ipeirotis found in his research that some workers at Mechanical Turk were already viewing their work on the site as full-time, serious work. One respondent in Ipeirotis's study said that he or she was "currently unemployed and so [I am] almost a full-time Turker. Although the rewards are rarely great, they build up rather quickly over time." By 2007, iStockphoto photographer Lisa Gagné was earning a six-figure income from sales of more than a half a million photos on the crowdsourced stock imagery site. And a few of the most successful Threadless designers make good incomes through their successes on Threadless and other graphic-design-competition sites.

The implications for this emerging professional crowd class are complex and worthy of study. As a generation of Americans comes of age in a depressed economy where steady full-time employment is hard to come by and retirement-age comforts like pensions and social security are uncertain, doing occasional or full-time crowdsourcing work may become common ways to make a living. If a professional crowd class emerges, will its members have their own sense of professional ethics, their own unions and collective bargaining power, or a shared sense of professional identity? Will curricula in schools adapt to teach students to become freelancers or crowd workers as legitimate professional options, or will there be organized resistance to crowdsourcing applications in way that no-spec creative workers have banded together?

Research into this new professional reality will be needed. This research may come from the disciplines of labor studies, leisure studies, and organizational communication, which have already contributed much to our understanding of professionalism and work-life balance. Management scholars will need to take up the economic questions of transient, ad-hoc crowd labor, and human-resource scholars and lawyers will need to consider crowd workers' legal relationships to organizations and the tax and benefit implications. The rise of crowdsourcing presents an interesting set of challenges for organizations, workers, and society that need to be addressed by scholarly research and practical insight.

GLOSSARY

citizen science
The performance of scientific research tasks by amateurs, hobbyists, and other individuals whose primary profession is not scientific research.

collective intelligence
A phenomenon where groups of people working together or taken in the aggregate become collectively intelligent as an entity.

crowd
An online community of individuals engaged in a crowdsourcing activity.

crowdfunding
The use of an online community to bring an idea or product to market through collective funding by several donors in the community.

crowdslapping
A crowd's resistance, within a crowdsourcing activity or a community space, to a crowdsourcer or a crowdsourcing activity.

crowdsourcer
An organization that operates a crowdsourcing application.

crowdsourcing
Using an online, distributed problem-solving and production model to leverage the collective intelligence of online communities to serve specific organizational goals.

distributed computing
The decomposition of a computing problem across a network to individual computers or nodes for processing.

human computation
The application of the principles of distributed computing to a network of human agents or nodes to process information that requires human intelligence.

human intelligence tasks (HITs)
Tasks that are simple for humans to perform but significantly more difficult for a computer to perform.

marginality in problem solving
The effect of those on the margins of a problem-solving domain who bring diverse problem-solving heuristics and experiences to bear on a problem.

microtasks
Small tasks that can be accomplished easily by humans, often work that contributes to a larger job that has been decomposed and distributed to many individual laborers.

online community management
In the context of an organization, project, or brand, the professional work of building and sustaining online communities around an organization, project, or brand.

open innovation
The strategic inclusion of external stakeholders in the innovation process of an organization.

participatory culture
The culture of content creation, sharing, and interaction that is fostered by the Internet, especially recent social media technologies and social networking sites.

user-generated content
In the context of the Internet, text or multimedia content that has been produced and distributed by Internet users online.

user innovation
A method where organizations incorporate the ideas and modifications to existing product iterations from users of a product.

wisdom of crowds
The phenomenon where groups of individuals outperform individuals who work alone to solve a problem.

FURTHER READINGS

Acar, Oguz Ali, and Jan van den Ende. 2011. Motivation, Reward Size and Contribution in Idea Crowdsourcing. Aalborg, Denmark. http://www2.druid.dk/conferences/viewpaper.php?id=502498&cf=47.

Allen, Naomi, Andrea Caillas, Jason Deveau-Rosen, Jason Kreps, Thomas Lemmo, Joseph Merante, Michael Murphy, Kaydi Osowski, Christopher Wong, and Mark Webbink. 2009. Peer-to-Patent Second Anniversary Report. Center for Patent Innovations at New York Law School. http://dotank.nyls.edu/communitypatent/CPI_P2P_YearTwo_hi.pdf.

Alt, F., A. S. Shirazi, A. Schmidt, U. Kramer, and Z. Nawaz. 2010. Location-based Crowdsourcing: Extending Crowdsourcing to the Real World. In *NordiCHI 2010 Proceedings*. New York: Association for Computing Machinery.

Anonymous n.d. About Apps for Healthy Kids. *Apps for Health Kids.* http://www.appsforhealthykids.com/#about.

Atkinson, Gail M., and David J. Wald. 2007. "Did You Feel It?" Intensity Data: A Surprisingly Good Measure of Earthquake Ground Motion. *Seismological Research Letters* 78 (3):362–368.

Benkler, Yochai. 2006. *The Wealth of Networks: How Social Production Transforms Markets and Freedom.* New Haven, CT: Yale University Press.

Boudreau, Kevin J., and Karim R. Lakhani. 2009. How to Manage Outside Innovation. *MIT Sloan Management Review* 50 (4):69–76.

Brabham, Daren C. 2007. Faces in the Crowd: Brett Snider. *Crowdsourcing: Tracking the Rise of the Amateur* (blog). http://crowdsourcing.typepad.com/cs/2007/03/faces_in_the_cr.html.

Brabham, Daren C. 2008a. Crowdsourcing as a Model for Problem Solving: An Introduction and Cases. *Convergence: The International Journal of Research into New Media Technologies* 14 (1):75–90.

Brabham, Daren C. 2008b. Moving the Crowd at iStockphoto: The Composition of the Crowd and Motivations for Participation in a Crowdsourcing Application. *First Monday* 13 (6). http://firstmonday.org/htbin/cgiwrap/bin/ojs/index.php/fm/article/view/2159/1969.

Brabham, Daren C. 2009. Crowdsourcing the Public Participation Process for Planning Projects. *Planning Theory* 8 (3):242–262.

Brabham, Daren C. 2010. Moving the Crowd at Threadless: Motivations for Participation in a Crowdsourcing Application. *Information Communication and Society* 13 (8):1122–1145.

Brabham, Daren C. 2012a. Crowdsourcing: A Model for Leveraging Online Communities. In *The Participatory Cultures Handbook*, ed. Aaron Delwiche and Jennifer Jacobs Henderson, 120–129. New York: Routledge.

Brabham, Daren C. 2012b. Motivations for Participation in a Crowdsourcing Application to Improve Public Engagement in Transit Planning. *Journal of Applied Communication Research* 40 (3):307–328.

Brabham, Daren C. 2012c. The Myth of Amateur Crowds: A Critical Discourse Analysis of Crowdsourcing Coverage. *Information Communication and Society* 15 (3):394–410.

Brito, Jerry. 2008. Hack, Mash, and Peer: Crowdsourcing Government Transparency. *Columbia Science and Technology Law Review* 9:119–157.

Campbell, Lisa. 2009. Dotmocracy: Crowdsourcing, Mashups, and Social Change. http://www.mobilerevolutions.org/Dotmocracy.pdf.

Eagle, N. 2009. Txteagle: Mobile Crowdsourcing. *Lecture Notes in Computer Science* 5623:447–456.

Frey, Karsten, Christian Lüthje, and Simon Haag. 2011. Whom Should Firms Attract to Open Innovation Platforms? The Role of Knowledge Diversity and Motivation. *Long Range Planning* 44:397–420.

Fritz, Steffen, Ian McCallum, Christian Schill, Christoph Perher, Roland Grillmayer, Frédéric Achard, Florian Kraxner, and Michael Obersteineer. 2009. Geo-Wiki.org: The Use of Crowdsourcing to Improve Global Land Cover. *Remote Sensing* 1 (3):345–354.

Gegenhuber, Thomas, and Marko Hrelja. 2012. Broadcast Search in Innovation Contests: Case for Hybrid Models. In *Collective Intelligence 2012: Proceedings*, ed. Thomas W. Malone and Luis von Ahn. Cambridge, MA: eprint arXiv:1204.2991. http://arxiv.org/ftp/arxiv/papers/1204/1204.3343.pdf.

Ipeirotis, Panagiotis G., Foster Provost, and Jing Wang. 2010. Quality Management on Amazon Mechanical Turk. In *Proceedings of the ACM SIGKDD*

Workshop on Human Computation, ed. Raman Chandrasekar, Ed Chi, Max Chickering, Panagiotis G. Ipeirotis, Winter Mason, Foster Provost, Jenn Tam, and Luis von Ahn, 64–67. New York: Association for Computing Machinery.

Kamensky, John. 2009. Using Crowdsourcing in Government. *IBM Center for the Business of Government Blog*. http://bizgov.wordpress.com/2009/09/16/using-crowdsourcing-in-government.

Kaufmann, Nicolas, Thimo Schulze, and Daniel Veit. 2011. More Than Fun and Money: Worker Motivation in Crowdsourcing—A Study on Mechanical Turk. In *Proceedings of the Seventeenth Americas Conference on Information Systems*, paper 340. Berkeley, CA: Digital Commons, Berkeley Electronic Press. http://aisel.aisnet.org/amcis2011_submissions/340.

Kessler, Sarah. 2011. Crowdsourcing Helps Holocaust Survivors Find Answers. *Mashable* (blog). http://mashable.com/2011/05/23/holocaust-museum-crowdsourcing.

Kleeman, F., G. G. Voss, and K. Rieder. 2008. Un(der)paid Innovators: The Commercial Utilization of Consumer Work through Crowdsourcing. *Science, Technology and Innovation Studies* 4 (1):5–26.

Lakhani, Karim R. 2008. *InnoCentive.com (A). Harvard Business School Case*. Cambridge, MA: Harvard Business School.

Lakhani, Karim R., and Zahra Kanji. 2008. *Threadless: The Business of Community. Harvard Business School Multimedia/Video Case*. Cambridge, MA: Harvard Business School.

Lakhani, Karim R., and Jill A. Panetta. 2007. The Principles of Distributed Innovation. *Innovations: Technology, Governance, Globalization* 2 (3):97–112.

La Vecchia, Gioacchino, and Antonio Cisternino. 2010. Collaborative Workforce, Business Process Crowdsourcing as an Alternative of BPO. *Lecture Notes in Computer Science* 6385:425–430.

Lips, M., and A. Rapson. 2010. Exploring Public Recordkeeping Behaviors in Wiki-Supported Public Consultation Activities in the New Zealand Public Sector. In *Proceedings of the Forty-third Hawaii International Conference on System Sciences*, ed. R. H. Sprague Jr. Los Alamitos, CA: IEEE Computer Society.

Messina, Michael Joseph. 2012. Crowdsourcing for Transit-Oriented Planning Projects: A Case Study of "inTeractive Somerville." MA thesis, Tufts University, Medford, MA.

Muthukumaraswamy, Karthika. 2010. When the Media Meet Crowds of Wisdom: How Journalists Are Tapping into Audience Expertise and Manpower for the Processes of Newsgathering. *Journalism Practice* 4 (1):48–65.

Noveck, Beth Simone. 2006. "Peer to Patent": Collective Intelligence, Open Review, and Patent Reform. *Harvard Journal of Law and Technology* 20 (1):123–262.

Noveck, Beth Simone. 2009. *Wiki Government: How Technology Can Make Government Better, Democracy Stronger, and Citizens More Powerful*. Washington, DC: Brookings Institution Press.

Okolloh, O. 2009. Ushahidi, or "Testimony": Web 2.0 Tools for Crowdsourcing Crisis Information. *Participatory Learning and Action* 59 (1):65–70.

Piyathasanan, Bhuminan, Paul Patterson, Ko De Ruyter, and Christine Mathies. 2011. Social Identity and Motivation for Creative Crowsourcing and Their Influence on Value Creation for the Firm. In *Australia New Zealand Marketing Academy Conference 2011 Proceedings*, ed. Martin MacCarthy. Perth, Australia: Edith Cowan University. http://anzmac.org/conference/2011/Papers%20 by%20Presenting%20Author/Piyathasana,%20Bhuminan%20Paper%20277 .pdf.

Powazek, Derek. 2007. Exploring the Dark Side of Crowdsourcing. *Wired*, July 11. http://www.wired.com/techbiz/media/news/2007/07/tricksters.

Siddique, Haroon. 2011. Mob Rule: Iceland Crowdsources Its Next Constitution: Country Recovering from Collapse of Its Banks and Government Is Using Social Media to Get Citizens to Share Their Ideas. *The Guardian*, June 9. http://www.guardian.co.uk/world/2011/jun/09/iceland-crowdsourcing-con stitution-facebook?CMP=twt_gu.

Stewart, Osamuyimen, Juan M. Huerta, and Melissa Sader. 2009. Designing Crowdsourcing Community for the Enterprise. In *Proceedings of the ACM SIG-KDD Workshop on Human Computation*, ed. Paul Bennett, Raman Chandrasekar, Max Chickering, Panos Ipeirotis, Edith Law, Anton Mityagin, Foster Provost, and Luis von Ahn, 50–53. New York: Association for Computing Machinery.

Tang, John C., Manuel Cebrian, Nicklaus A. Giacobe, Hyun-Woo Kim, Taemie Kim, and Douglas "Beaker" Wickert. 2011. Reflecting on the DARPA Red Balloon Challenge. *Communications of the ACM* 54 (4):78–85.

Trompette, P., V. Chanal, and C. Pelissier. 2008. Crowdsourcing as a Way to Access External Knowledge for Innovation: Control, Incentive and Coordination in Hybrid Forms of Innovation. In *Twenty-fourth EGOS Colloquium*. Amsterdam.

Urquhart, Emily S. 2012. Listening to the Crowd: A Content Analysis of Social Media Chatter about a Crowdsourcing Contest. BA honors thesis, University of North Carolina, Chapel Hill, NC.

Vukovic, Maja, and Claudio Bartolini. 2010. Towards a Research Agenda for Enterprise Crowdsourcing. *Lecture Notes in Computer Science* 6415:425–434.

Vukovic, Maja, Jim Laredo, and Sriram Rajagopal. 2010. Challenges and Experiences in Deploying Enterprise Crowdsourcing Service. *Lecture Notes in Computer Science* 6189:460–467.

BIBLIOGRAPHY

Amabile, Teresa M. 1998. How to Kill Creativity. *Harvard Business Review* (October):77–87.

Benkler, Yochai. 2002. Coase's Penguin, or, Linux and *The Nature of the Firm*. *Yale Law Journal* 112 (3):369–446.

Bluestein, Frayda. 2010. Free Speech Rights in Government Social Media Sites. *Coates' Canons: NC Local Government Law Blog*. http://canons.sog.unc .edu/?p=1970.

Bongard, Josh C., Paul D. H. Hines, Dylan Conger, Peter Hurd, and Zhenyu Lu. Forthcoming. Crowdsourcing Predictors of Behavioral Outcomes. *IEEE Transactions on Systems, Man, and Cybernetics. Part A, Systems and Humans*. http:// ieeexplore.ieee.org/search/searchresult.jsp?punumber=3468&searchWithin= bongard.

Brzozowski, Michael J., Thomas Sandholm, and Tad Hogg. 2009. Effects of Feedback and Peer Pressure on Contributions to Enterprise Social Media. In *Proceedings of the ACM 2009 International Conference on Supporting Group Work*, 61–70. New York: Association for Computing Machinery.

Carey, James W. 1989. *Communication as Culture: Essays on Media and Society*. Winchester, MA: Unwin Hyman.

Carr, Nicholas. 2010. A Typology of Crowds. *Rough Type* (blog). http://www .roughtype.com/?p=1346.

Chesbrough, Henry. 2003. *Open Innovation: The New Imperative for Creating and Profiting from Technology*. Boston: Harvard Business Press.

Davey, Neil. 2010. Ross Dawson: Six Tools to Kickstart Your Crowdsourcing Strategy. MyCustomer.com. http://www.mycustomer.com/topic/customer -intelligence/ross-dawson-six-tools-start-your-crowdsourcing-strategy/109914.

Deci, Edward L., and Richard M. Ryan. 1985. *Intrinsic Motivation and Self-determination in Human Behavior*. New York: Plenum.

Doty, D. Harold, and William H. Glick. 1994. Typologies as a Unique Form of Theory Building: Toward Improved Understanding and Modeling. *Academy of Management Review* 19 (2):230–251.

Dunbar, Kevin. 1998. Problem Solving. In *A Companion to Cognitive Science*, ed. W. Bechtel and G. Graham, 289–298. London: Blackwell. http://www.utsc.utoronto.ca/~dunbarlab/pubpdfs/probsolv2.pdf.

Estellés-Arolas, Enrique, and Fernando González-Ladrón-de-Guevara. 2012. Towards an Integrated Crowdsourcing Definition. *Journal of Information Science* 38 (2):189–200.

Fournier, Valérie. 1999. The Appeal to "Professionalism" as a Disciplinary Mechanism. *Sociological Review* 47 (2):280–307.

Gartner, Inc. 2012. Gartner Says by 2014, 10–15 Percent of Social Media Reviews to Be Fake, Paid for by Companies. Gartner Research. http://www.gartner.com/it/page.jsp?id=2161315.

Geiger, David, Stefan Seedorf, Thimo Schulze, Robert C. Nickerson, and Martin Schader. 2011. Managing the Crowd: Towards a Taxonomy of Crowdsourcing Processes. In *Proceedings of the Seventeenth Americas Conference on Information Systems*, paper 430. Detroit, MI.

Ghosh, R. A. 1998. *FM* Interview with Linus Torvalds: What Motivates Free Software Developers? *First Monday* 3 (3). http://firstmonday.org/htbin/cgiwrap/bin/ojs/index.php/fm/article/view/1475/1390.

Goldcorp. 2001. Goldcorp Challenge Winners! Goldcorp Challenge. http://www.goldcorpchallenge.com/challenge1/winnerslist/challeng2.pdf.

Hong, Lu, and Scott E. Page. 2001. Problem Solving by Heterogeneous Agents. *Journal of Economic Theory* 97:123–163.

Horovitz, Bruce. 2009. "Two Nobodies from Nowhere" Craft Winning Super Bowl Ad. *USA Today*, December 31. http://www.usatoday.com/money/advertising/admeter/2009admeter.htm.

Howe, Jeff. 2006a. Mission Statement. *Crowdsourcing: Tracking the Rise of the Amateur* (blog). http://www.crowdsourcing.com/cs/2006/05/hi_my_name_is_j.html.

Howe, Jeff. 2006b. Pure, Unadulterated (and Scalable) Crowdsourcing. *Crowdsourcing: Tracking the Rise of the Amateur* (blog). http://crowdsourcing.typepad.com/cs/2006/06/pure_unadultera.html.

Howe, Jeff. 2006c. The Rise of Crowdsourcing. *Wired*, June. http://www.wired.com/wired/archive/14.06/crowds.html.

Howe, Jeff. 2007. Did Assignment Zero Fail? A Look Back, and Lessons Learned. *Wired*, July 16. http://www.wired.com/techbiz/media/news/2007/07/assignment_zero_final.

Howe, Jeff. 2008. *Crowdsourcing: Why the Power of the Crowd Is Driving the Future of Business*. New York: Crown.

Huberman, Bernardo A., Daniel M. Romero, and Fang Wu. 2009. Crowdsourcing, Attention and Productivity. *Journal of Information Science* 35 (6):758–765.

International Association of Business Communicators. n.d. IABC Code of Ethics for Professional Communicators. International Association of Business Communicators. http://www.iabc.com/about/code.htm.

Ipeirotis, Panagiotis G. 2010. Analyzing the Amazon Mechanical Turk Marketplace. *XRDS: Crossroads, The ACM Magazine for Students* 17 (2):16–21.

Jenkins, Henry. 2006. *Convergence Culture: Where Old and New Media Collide*. New York: New York University Press.

Jenkins, Henry, with Ravi Purushotma, Margaret Weigel, Katie Clinton, and Alice J. Robison. 2006a. *Confronting the Challenges of Participatory Culture: Media Education for the Twenty-first Century*. White paper. Chicago: MacArthur Foundation. http://newmedialiteracies.org/files/working/NMLWhitePaper.pdf.

Jeppesen, Lars Bo, and Karim R. Lakhani. 2010. Marginality and Problem-solving Effectiveness in Broadcast Search. *Organization Science* 21 (5):1016–1033.

Kazai, Gabriella, Jaap Kamps, and Natasa Milic-Frayling. 2011. Worker Types and Personality Traits in Crowdsourcing Relevance Labels. In *Proceedings of the Twentieth ACM International Conference on Information and Knowledge Management*, 1941–1944. New York: Association for Computing Machinery.

Knoke, David, and Christine Wright-Isak. 1982. Individual Motives and Organizational Incentive Systems. *Research in the Sociology of Organizations* 1:209–254.

Lakhani, Karim R., Lars Bo Jeppesen, Peter A. Lohse, and Jill A. Panetta. 2007. *The Value of Openness in Scientific Problem Solving*. Harvard Business School Working Paper. http://www.hbs.edu/research/pdf/07-050.pdf.

Lakhani, Karim R., and Robert G. Wolf. 2005. Why Hackers Do What They Do: Understanding Motivation and Effort in Free/Open Source Software Projects. In *Perspectives on Free and Open Source Software*, ed. Joseph Feller, Brian

Fitzgerald, Scott A. Hissam, and Karim R. Lakhani, 3–22. Cambridge, MA: MIT Press.

Lessig, Lawrence. 2004. *Free Culture: How Big Media Uses Technology and the Law to Lock Down Culture and Control Creativity*. New York: Penguin Press.

Lévy, Pierre. 1995. *Collective Intelligence: Mankind's Emerging World in Cyberspace*. Trans. Robert Bononno. New York: Plenum.

Lietsala, Katri, and Atte Joutsen. 2007. Hang-a-Rounds and True Believers: A Case Analysis of the Roles and Motivational Factors of the *Star Wreck* Fans. In *MindTrek 2007 Conference Proceedings*, ed. Artur Lugmayr, Katri Lietsala, and Jan Kallenbach, 25–30. Tampere, Finland: Tampere University of Technology.

Liu, Su-Houn, Hsiu-Li Liao, and Yuan-Tai Zeng. 2007. Why People Blog: An Expectancy Theory Analysis. *Issues in Information Systems* 8 (2):232–237.

Martineau, Eric. 2012. A Typology of Crowdsouricng Participation Styles. M.S. thesis, Concordia University, Montreal. http://spectrum.library.concordia.ca/973811/1/Martineau_MSc_Winter_2012.pdf.

NO!SPEC. n.d. About NO!SPEC. http://www.no-spec.com/about/.

Nov, Oded. 2007. What Motivates Wikipedians? *Communications of the ACM* 50 (11):60–64.

Nov, Oded, Mor Naaman, and Chen Ye. 2008. What Drives Content Tagging: The Case of Photos on Flickr. In *Proceedings of the Twenty-sixth Annual SIGCHI Conference on Human Factors in Computing Systems*, ed. Margaret Burnett, Maria Francesca Costabile, Tiziana Catarci, Boris de Ruyter, Desney Tan, Mary Czerwinski, and Arnie Lund, 1097–1100. New York: Association for Computing Machinery.

Noveck, Beth Simone. 2003. Designing Deliberative Democracy in Cyberspace: The Role of the Cyber-lawyer. *Boston University Journal of Science and Technology Law* 9 (1):1–91.

Page, Scott E. 2007. *The Difference: How the Power of Diversity Creates Better Groups, Firms, Schools, and Societies*. Princeton, NJ: Princeton University Press.

Perry, James L., and Lois Recascino Wise. 1990. The Motivational Bases of Public Service. *Public Administration Review* 50 (3):367–373.

Post, Robert C. 1995. *Constitutional Domains: Democracy, Community, Management*. Cambridge, MA: Harvard University Press.

Public Relations Society of America. n.d. Public Relations Society of America (PRSA) Member Code of Ethics. Public Relations Society of America. http://www.prsa.org/AboutPRSA/Ethics/CodeEnglish/index.html.

Ritzer, George. 1975. Professionalization, Bureaucratization and Rationalization: The Views of Max Weber. *Social Forces* 53 (4):627–634.

Rogstadius, Jakob, Vassilis Kostakos, Aniket Kittur, Boris Smus, Jim Laredo, and Maja Vukovic. 2011. An Assessment of Intrinsic and Extrinsic Motivation on Task Performance in Crowdsourcing Markets. In *Proceedings of the Fifth International Conference on Weblogs and Social Media*, 321–328. Menlo Park, CA: AAAI Press.

Salminen, Juho. 2012. Collective Intelligence in Humans: A Literature Review. In *Collective Intelligence 2012: Proceedings*, ed. Thomas W. Malone and Luis von Ahn. Cambridge, MA: eprint arXiv:1204.2991. http://arxiv.org/ftp/arxiv/papers/1204/1204.3401.pdf.

Schenk, Eric, and Claude Guittard. 2011. Towards a Characterization of Crowdsourcing Practices. *Journal of Innovation Economics* 7 (1):93–107.

Suler, John R. 2004. The Online Disinhibition Effect. *Cyberpsychology and Behavior* 7:321–326.

Surowiecki, James. 2004. *The Wisdom of Crowds: Why the Many Are Smarter Than the Few and How Collective Wisdom Shapes Business, Economies, Societies, and Nations*. New York: Doubleday.

Terranova, Tiziana. 2004. *Network Culture: Politics for the Information Age*. London: Pluto Press.

Terwiesch, Christian, and Yi Xu. 2008. Innovation Contests, Open Innovation, and Multiagent Problem Solving. *Management Science* 54 (9):1529–1543.

Touschner, Peter. 2011. Subverting New Media for Profit: How Online Social Media "Black Markets" Violate Section 5 of the Federal Trade Commission Act. *Hastings Science and Technology Law Journal* 3 (1):165–192.

US White House. n.d. About the SAVE Award. US White House. http://www.whitehouse.gov/save-award/about.

Van Dijck, José, and David Nieborg. 2009. Wikinomics and Its Discontents: A Critical Analysis of Web 2.0 Business Manifestos. *New Media and Society* 11 (5):855–874.

Villarroel, J. Andrei, and Filipa Reis. 2010. Intra-corporate Crowdsourcing (ICC): Leveraging upon Rank and Site Marginality for Innovation. Paper presented at CrowdConf 2010: The World's First Conference on the Future of Distributed Work, San Francisco. http://www.crowdconf2010.com/images/finalpapers/villarroel.pdf.

Von Ahn, Luis, Ben Maurer, Colin McMillen, David Abraham, and Manuel Blum. 2008. reCAPTCHA: Human-based Character Recognition via Web Security Measures. *Science* 321 (5895): 1465–1468.

Von Hippel, Eric. 2005. *Democratizing Innovation*. Cambridge, MA: MIT Press.

Wiggins, Andrea, and Kevin Crowston. 2011. From Conservation to Crowdsourcing: A Typology of Citizen Science. In *Proceedings of the Forty-fourth Hawaii International Conference on Systems Science*, ed. R. H. Sprague, Jr. Los Alamitos, CA: IEEE Computer Society.

Wu, Fang, Dennis M. Wilkinson, and Bernardo Huberman. 2009. Feedback Loops of Attention in Peer Production. In *Proceedings of the 2009 IEEE International Conference on Social Computing*, 409–415. Los Alamitos, CA: IEEE Computer Society.

Zerfass, Ansgar, Stephan Fink, and Anne Linke. 2011. Social Media Governance: Regulatory Frameworks as Drivers of Success in Online Communications. In *Fourteenth International Public Relations Research Conference Proceedings*, ed. Linjuan Rita Men and Melissa D. Dodd, 1026–1046. Coral Gables, FL: Institute for Public Relations. http://www.instituteforpr.org/wp-content/uploads/14th-IPRRC-Proceedings.pdf.

Zheng, Haichao, Dahui Li, and Wenhua Hou. 2011. Task Design, Motivation, and Participation in Crowdsourcing Contests. *International Journal of Electronic Commerce* 15 (4):57–88.

INDEX